STAYING MOTIVATED

IN A WORLD OF INCREASING CHALLENGES

Book by
ALLEN STEBLE

Staying Motivated in a World of Increasing Challenges
Copyright © 2021 by Allen Steble

All rights reserved. No part of this publication may be reproduced, distributed, or transmitted in any form or by any means, including photocopying, recording, or other electronic or mechanical methods, without the prior written permission of the author, except in the case of brief quotations embodied in critical reviews and certain other non-commercial uses permitted by copyright law.

ISBN
978-1-956529-16-6 (Hardcover)
978-1-956529-04-3 (Paperback)
978-1-956529-03-6 (eBook)

Table of Contents

Foreward vii

The art of persistence 2
The right motivators 20
Keeping your eyes on the prize 36
Persevere to perspire, working hard at your goals 52
The race beyond the finish line 68
Rebuilding yourself from your design 80
Staying on the path of motivation 98

Foreward

Let me start by saying Thank you dear reader for choosing to engulf yourself in my book on staying motivated in a world of increasing challenges. I am by no means an expert or professional in any field so any advice I give in this book is based purely on my experiences, observations, and my journey up until this point. The reason I wrote this book was to serve as a reminder to myself and others that there are always reasons to stay motivated in whatever you set out to achieve and to provide encouragement to all those seeking it and who are actively struggling to stick it out and push to the end and beyond. To say that I struggle to stay motivated most of the time would be a gross understatement as I feel the constant resistance every day that wants to keep me from even getting out of bed in the morning and start an awesome day of moving forward. One of the main goals of this book is to challenge yourself to overcome one of the biggest killers of motivation, laziness, and procrastination. I am going to include challenges at the end of each chapter to help you solidify the main points contained within them and to help you grow in motivation as you read through this book.

Only you have the power to change yourself and push yourself to greater heights truly, and it is my keen desire to help you see that and hopefully help you to achieve a more motivated and positive mindset in achieving that goal. I highly encourage you to actively engage in the challenges at the end of each chapter, only one of these challenges should be attempted each week as you don't want to do too much all at once and overload yourself with excessive tasks. This book has the power to challenge your thinking habits and inspire you to become better each day; it will help you notice distractions and how to manage them, so your life does not become inundated with them. I will discuss the value in setting small and large goals and how to stay motivated to achieve the smaller ones one by one, so they can eventually form your primary goals. Once again though only you have the power to produce positive change in your life and you must be willing to put in whatever hard work is necessary to achieve that, obstacles are an inevitable, and they will always be there to test how badly you want what you say you want. I will guide you to persistence and help you to realize that truly just about anything is possible with the right mindset and steps.

There's a chance that not everything in this book will resonate with you, and that is perfectly fine, we are all different in many aspects of our lives. We have our unique challenges and situation, but it is my firm hope that you will gain same hidden valuable gems from the chapters in this book and hopefully find new ways to think about overcoming obstacles and achieving goals in various aspects of your day-to-day progression. The only thing I do ask is to read this book with an open mind to see that there are many paths in your life that will reveal themselves once you reveal your inner potential, this book will help you to find it if you truly listen and aspire to improve your journey. You will discover that staying motivated can be very challenging in this world of distractions and constant technological affluence, but it can also be easy if you have the right formula to fuel it and the right awareness to identify the roadblocks that will inevitably manifest before you. We will learn about certain mindsets and how they affect motivation and how to cultivate the ones that keep you in a state of higher motivation.

You will find that motivation is a choice and, your passions and goals create it. It is also a muscle that with consistent exercise in discipline and self-awareness, it is a quality that grows with you as you get closer to your completion point in any task. We will also discuss why it is important to create small goals that contribute to a larger purpose rather than measure the portion of the larger goal as an incomplete entity. Motivation is a sense of clarity that is backed by action, so downtime is important in your daily grind, as rest creates clarity. Find your motivation and a sense of purpose so you too can see what lies beyond the woes of everyday existence and discover that personal meaning in your own life.

It is important to state too that often the cause of a lack of motivation may be due to a lingering medical condition causing fatigue and low mood, issues such as diabetes or any thyroid condition. In most cases, however, mental illness can take the biggest toll on your drive and motivation levels, so it is vital that you seek the appropriate professional help from your health care provider in managing such disorders. If you ignore this, no matter how much of these guidelines you apply you will still be at a significant disadvantage as your overall health and wellbeing are the result of your mental and physical health both being at optimal levels. This book's aim is to help people to get to the next level in a world inundated with distraction, addictions, and instant gratifications. Help yourself first by making sure that you are overall healthy and balanced; then you will be ahead of the curve in taking your motivation and enthusiasm to the next level or success.

Chapter 1

Staying Motivated in a World of Increasing Challenges

The art of persistence

> "A determined person
> doesn't find it hard to succeed,
> they find it hard
> to stop trying"
> Allen Steble

Staying motivated is one of life's greatest challenges. Every year hundreds of millions of people make hundreds of millions of well-intentioned resolutions. These resolutions encompass a vast scope of goals, some of the most common including daily exercise, weight loss, eating more natural foods regularly, reading a certain number of books or pursuing a dream career and perhaps embarking on a particular field of study. These resolutions symbolize a greater need in each of us to become the best person we aspire to be in this world and are the first steps to grow into who we came here to be. Why do most of us fail to follow through on these goals? Usually one thing is to blame, a lack of motivation!

Why write a book about it? This is very important to me because we live in a day and age where staying motivated is becoming increasingly more challenging. Many people are finding themselves in situations where they want to quit and give up, myself often included. Deep down, many of us don't feel like we know what we want, or we know what we want but believe it's too hard to achieve. Whatever your reasons it's clear that with the new challenges we all face in daily life now it is so important that we stay motivated and work towards our end games. So many people want the easy life, but if success were easy, then everybody would have it and be satisfied with their lives. Sadly, many of us are not. Being successful is a constant uphill battle that is very often hard to achieve and requires motivation, and the right motivation at that, to achieve. This book aims at pointing you in the right direction and helping you to create better habits to stay motivated. Success is also subjective and personal, think about it! Would you rather be a miserable millionaire or a joyful person of little means? How you measure your success is up to you at the end of the day and only you can decide what that success looks and feels like, ask yourself some of the questions below and see how you fair in terms of mental success and general contentment with the life you have.

Do I wake up in the morning with almost no energy?
Do I find it almost impossible to get out of bed most days?
Do I feel unmotivated with achieving my goals?
Do I feel like I know I could be so much more
but don't know how to get there?

These are common complaints from a vast majority of people I speak to regarding their unique circumstances.

Persistence is at the forefront of success, the greatest innovators, athletes, scientists, writers, entrepreneur, and leaders have all had one thing in common, the ability to persevere, to keep trying even when the odds were stacked against them. What was different though? What made them want it that much more than everyone else? To answer this Question requires more than just a mere examination of the lives of these extraordinary people, it requires a look at ourselves, a deep look into a human being at his or her very core.

SELF IMAGE

Self-image has become a fundamental standpoint in today's society, look at how many magazines are produced every week presenting supermodels with "the perfect body" showcasing on the catwalk, in vogue, playboy, woman's day and a multitude of other smoothly printed magazines. A man is judged outwardly on his physical stamina, how large his biceps are, how toned his abs are. How much he can bench press, or how much money he makes. People don't only buy into these ideals, many live by their sky-high expectations as if that is the meaning of their very existence.

So how does self-image come in to play when talking about staying motivated? How one sees him/herself plays a monumental role in staying motivated, for the moment you place vague and shallow labels on yourself, you in effect control your potential from the standpoint of societal expectations. For instance, say a man of average height is aspiring to play professional basketball, knowing he is below standard height for most players would likely be affected by his self-image. I am too short (label). Therefore, basketball may not be the best career choice (hesitation). This hesitation now causes a great obstacle for this individual. Yes, he might not be great in height and that will affect his ability to dunk unless he climbs up Shaquille O'Neil on the court.

This is still dictated by his dependence on the ideals of the populous. If there was ever a reason to quit something you love, this is not how you want to go about it. So, you're not the tallest player on the team; what you lack in height, you likely make up for in speed, endurance, and determination, which are even greater than inherited physical traits. The great become great because they use what they have to create an advantage and develop the qualities that those with born talents usually take for granted, such as the ability to push above and beyond what others 'expect' from them.

Everybody must start somewhere, although we are shaped by and large by our environment, we are the masters of our vessel, we in effect mould ourselves to a greater degree than our environment. Rather than being influenced by our environment, we should focus on inventing our ideal environment through the process of radical momentum and starting with positive and purposeful changes at a consistent level to get the momentum rolling. In my experience, I have found out that eating more natural food is key to creating the habit of forming large and concrete change. Once the ball started rolling consistently, I could see positive results, and, these will roll into other aspects of your life such as your organizational habits, fitness goals and future choices.

THE BREAKING POINT

The breaking point is a time in your life where you are tired of the results you are producing and know that it's time for a change, it's almost a matter of life or death, and the feeling of staying in the same place is more painful than the risk of change. For many it's the point where they have been bullied for so long, they no longer feel any ounce of self-respect because of the constant barrage of harsh words that have penetrated their mind, or the chronically obese man who has just been told if he doesn't make a change now he risks a major heart attack in the next 6 months. Now is the time for decisive change because there is a strong enough MUST. This must be achieved either genuinely or artificially, most people who obtain it genuinely have reached a stage where change is vital for their physical or emotional survival such as being pre-diabetic from poor dietary habits or being on the verge of emphysema due to the relief that comes from the constant drag of daily cigarettes. Most people, unfortunately, fall into this category where though it is not too late, they could have improved their situation by acting sooner.

A few achieve it artificially. For some reason, they imagine what their life will be like if they continue their current course. They imagine the harm of putting on those extra few kilos that tip them towards obesity or diabetes. This imagined pain has the same psychological effect in that it tricks your brain into believing that the situation is real, your brain can not notice the difference. They plan their steps ahead of the calamity and safeguard themselves, taking the necessary steps to correct their issue before it becomes more problematic down the line. This is where true success lies. Staying motivated requires visualizing the finished product, seeing your current situation now and what it will embody in the near or distant future.

"I have gained 25kg in 1 year since eating pizza 3 times a week (my current observation). As a result, I now border on type 2 diabetes. Therefore, I now must act for my life is at stake. (Genuine must). I have gained 5 kg in the last 3 months eating pizza 3 times a week if I continue at this rate, I may be 20kg overweight by the end of the year. If I act now, I can reduce that risk and choose a healthier lifestyle (artificial must). See the benefit of this reasoning?

The person observed their situation, realized they don't want to continue down that path, then calculated the risk of their current lifestyle by multiplying that number to get an end of year result. The prudent see danger and take refuge, but the simple keep going and pay the penalty, Proverbs 22:3. Don't be simple, be wise and take notice of your direction in life and make the positive changes you know you need to make now to improve your circumstances.

This is simple yet profound, for the person with the strongest reason for "why" they must achieve something is the most likely to "persist" in the "how to achieve" this area. For this reason, too, those who see themselves as winners and champions will always be more successful than those with a poor self-image because the mindset is already on the prize as if it already belongs to them 100%. This is the fundamental difference between the wealthy and the poor, the so-called scarcity or poverty mindset. The mind works as a sort of self-fulfilling prophecy magnet, you send out messages to the universe, and it replies like sonar reflecting the signals you sent out back to you, so make sure you're sending out the right ones, the kind that moves you closer towards your goal.

This is where creating a need to succeed vs. wanting to succeed come into play. Everyone has needs and wants; the difference again is the attitude in going after those things. We need food, shelter, and clothing, so instinctually we strive for those things first and will always find a way to fulfil them. Wants, on the other hand, take second priority as they are not essential but rather "optional enjoyments" like a chocolate bar or glass of wine after a long day at work. This is not to say that being materially affluent or any other compulsion is a necessity, far from it. However, we are a collection of our mental, physical, emotional and spiritual selves. If anyone of these is suffering then we are not complete, it must, therefore, become a necessity to be rich in all aspects of our lives, that is what is needed to acquire true success.

HOW TO BECOME RICH IN ALL ASPECTS OF YOUR LIFE

The rich man thinks abundance, feels abundance, lives abundance and is abundance. He has no wants, he only has what he is, and he is in a constant state of gratitude in the face of every and any situation. Although he realizes life is no smooth road, he is aware that there are no mistakes and that whatever may or may not take place, is only another steppingstone towards his ultimate goals, and true calling, and where he currently is in his own life is a direct result of his thoughts, feelings, actions, and choices that led him there, this is simple cause and effect, and we are all subjects to it either knowingly or ignorantly. We become rich in any aspect of our lives by thinking richly, feeling richly, acting in rich ways, and making rich choices.

A rich man is not rich purely because of hard work and wise investment but is rich from his state of mind and amalgamation of every area of his life that merits his attention. Rich people invest in themselves and thus tap into the infinite potential that exists from knowing and living their passions, it is more than mere cliché, and it is a clear reality to adopt this mentality. Look at Bill Gates, the inventor of Microsoft, and one of the world's richest men. He is rich because he followed his passion and thus it became his purpose. He had faith and confidence in himself and his abilities that he could add value to the world, and he did. Most of us invest in other people's ideals and therefore become slaves to their theologies, caught up in a loop of routine and consistency that dull the mind into blind submission. We should be questioning why we are following this way or that way, or ask ourselves is there a better way? How can we escape this routine? And more importantly, how can we live our passion to make us rich in all areas?

There is no such thing as a rich follower, see for yourself, following implies you do not know your own way, or you lack the capacity to find it, therefore you follow someone else. If you are rich, it is because you knew your way like Bill Gates did, or Warren Buffet did, or Steve Jobs did, or the many others who followed their passions. If you want to become rich you must become a leader of yourself and not a follower of anyone else. That fact that others may choose to follow you is only testament to your capabilities as a leader and a person who follows their passion. It is better to fail fifty times trying to lead than accept once that you are nothing more than a follower to the ideals of someone who knows nor cares even a tiny bit about your dreams or passions, yet how do you really know what your passion or passions are?

What is Passion?

What do you think of when you think of passion? Passion can refer to fierce love, aggression or perhaps a flaring feeling of excitement pulsing to explode from within. However, you choose to view it doesn't matter, what matters is its life-changing potential. Most people do not realize the passion that they have until later in their life. When we are younger, and life is generally simpler we have the freedom to play and have fun guilt free, no real responsibilities to weigh us down, sadly as we age, we seem to lose this sense of spontaneity and passion in taking risks to get what we want. In adult life it becomes a matter of making the time and prioritizing between the fifteen different mundane tasks we feel obligated to do. We are our own worst enemies when it comes to holding back from doing what we love or even giving it a fair go.

Thus, goes the man who has all the money in the world, but no passion has significantly less than the man who lives his passion and has very little money because the investment of self is where the universe's abundance lies and generously rewards whoever follows through on its wise calling. For without passion life is a blank canvas of monotony waiting to be sold to a lifeless soul but never does, for it is grey and meaningless, whereas the man who embraces passion with every ounce of his being is just like a beautiful painting of dancing colours that everyone wants a share, it has meaning and depth that explode with gratitude. The point herein is those who do what they love and live their passion become rich due to the abundance of energy they exude through the freedom to be themselves and none other. So, what holds most people back from living their passions?

Distractions

Life is full of distractions, everyone knows that. It always has been and always will. They teach us a valuable lesson though; they act as a filter to what matters most to us. Work gets in the way; financial difficulty gets in the way; life gets in the way. Once again it comes down to this, you must decide what is important to you, remember if something is that valuable to you, then you **must** make time for it, no excuses! If you don't know what you like or are passionate about then designate time to think about it, meditate it over and try various things out until you feel the spark of passion ignite from the embers of self-exploration. For me what I have found helps a great deal is writing down a list of 10 or more things I like and then actively observing my emotional state at the time of thinking it, when I look at what I've written Down, how do I feel? Excited, mildly happy, moderately happy, passionate, over the moon, bored out of my mind, the fact is you will know very quickly what interests you and what doesn't. I evaluate from a level of 1 to 10, 1 being mind-numbingly tedious and 10 being I must do this now and not stop even for a coffee break. Be honest with yourself! You cannot trick yourself when it comes to matters of the heart. When you do find something be realistic about what distractions may get in the way and how you can logically get around them and don't forget to write these down and keep them somewhere you can revert to when you need to. Remember, living passionately is such an important.

Key to the journey of happiness it cannot be overstated enough. Many people fail to find their passion because they have started to ignore their inner voices for too long, to the point where the shouts of their hearts become muffled by the distractions of everyday life, don't let this be you, if you haven't found it yet, start listening to your emotions and find what it is that breathes fulfilment into your soul.

Passion is energy. Feel the power that comes from focusing on what excites you. Oprah Winfrey.

The four phases of defeat

There exist in the world a great many passion killers, just like there exist many persistence killers. These I will attempt to break down into 4 phases.

Phase One
Is it really what I want?

It is the 1-million-dollar question, what do "I want" regarding my goals? Is the "why" for achieving my goal great enough? Say you work for a company in office supplies and earn $35000 a year working full time. Now say you were offered a job manufacturing car parts for $38500 a year working full time but required an extra 30 minutes a day and more manual labour, is your "why" for choosing this job great enough to motivate radical change in leaving your current job for the extra few thousand a year, you may not think so. However, were it an opportunity to learn new skills in an exciting environment and offered substantial remuneration financially with prospects for career advancements you would probably leap fr the opportunity.

We are creatures of purpose and we like to find meaning in the activities we engage in. Why does a person run a marathon? Why does a person become a chef? Why does a person want to be a computer programmer? The key word here is "want." We are born and shaped with different desires, whether environmental or hereditary, yet we are born with fundamental differences from everyone else.

It's like enrolling in a college degree; you generally have 4 or more courses you can apply for in order of priority. Start with your desired course in the first position and then the next preferred and so on. Often deciding what exactly you want is a challenging task that will take time and focus figuring out and there are a lot of factors that determine what will make you Say, "this is what I want to do with my life." What are your strengths, what are you naturally talented at doing, what to people generally commend you for? When you look at something, how elated do you become? For me, I look at any word related to computers, games or health and fitness and I am energized.

Putting all nonsense aside let me say the only time I am persistent is when I am going after something I truly want, that's it. Visualize what you want and become so excited about it that it fills you with abundant joy. It'll make you work relentlessly towards it every day; you will find no excuse to prevent you from moving forward toward it, keep believing and persevering and it is only a matter of time before it will reveal itself to you when the time is right.

I write this book to tell you I firmly believe you can have what you want, the only obstacle is knowing what you 'ACTUALLY' want.

Phase Two
Do I believe I can get what I want?

This is where a LOT of people struggle and collapse in exhaustion, and many of us have been programmed from a young age that we should only go after modest things that are in our reach "You are only a C student so you should become a mechanic or you should just get a regular 9 to 5 job to support yourself... I say "to hell with that!", If I want something bad enough, that means anything then I am going after that shit whether anyone likes it or not or believes it or not! That is it, there is no other way about it, if you know what you want and are excited enough about it, then bloody well do it!

I spoke to several people asking them what they want to get out of life and what they would love to accomplish. Responses have varied from things such as "I want to be an" engineer, scientist, actor, etc. They have big dreams that are noteworthy. So, what are you doing now? "oh well I work at the local supermarket or at McDonald's taking orders full time. Then I would ask, why are you not studying in your dream field, and the typical well-thought-out reply is something along the lines of... "I am not smart enough, talented enough, good looking enough" (insert ridiculous excuse). Now I am going to say something that should be permanently ingrained in your mind...ready...

There is no excuse when it comes to your passions! Period!!! There are only obstacles that test your resolve in fulfilling said passions. If you own a house or car, I am sure you have had some problems with them from time to time, when you have those problems do you say, "ah crap, well the roof is leaking so I am going to live in the trash can from now on because at least it doesn't leak." That is in effect what we say when we give up on our dreams, we move from our luxurious home (vision) to the garbage can (mediocrity or worse).

When you have figured out your dream, always keep a physical reminder of it in visual sight, so you are constantly reminded of its power within you both when you wake up and before you go to sleep. It will drive itself into your subconscious so every time you see it, you will know you must take radical action to move closer toward it. Once you look at it enough, believing in its manifestation will yield into your subconscious mind over time to the point you will believe that it's an inevitable reality and it will be achieved with your persistence and unending resolve.

Phase Three
Accepting Mediocrity

Do you accept mediocrity in your life? For many years I answered yes to that nerve pinching question. I look back on those years and want to knock some sense into myself. Bad Career choices, relationships and down-right stupid decisions are on my list, and you probably have many of your regrets too, the fact is we all have our comfort zones, and they can be one of the most challenging obstacles to overcome. Think about it honestly with yourself, what truly successful person got to where they are in life by sitting on the couch drinking beer and watching football or playing video games until their eyes became dried apricots? The only way to move past mediocrity is to step outside of your comfort zone and take a cold shower so to speak.

One thing I have noticed recently is very profound. If I wake up in the morning feeling like dog excrement, sit at my computer desk and accept that today is going to be a lazy day filled with slacking off, that day comes to realization very quickly and becomes just that, if I make the conscious decision and stick by it and remain in my comfort zone there is no doubt, I will have one feeling at the end of that day... regret. The best days I have and can recall all start the same, with me saying I am going to step outside my comfort zone today and achieve something, even small, that I usually would not do or be comfortable with. Usually though once I start one task that makes me feel a little success, I immediately follow it up with other tasks and comfort zone-destroying tasks.

Think about it yourself, what have your most successful days felt like? What did you do? Then think how they began. Odds are your best moments have occurred outside your comfort zone, by breaking these consistently, key word there being consistently, you will very quickly break the curse of mediocrity and the tolerance of this nasty word.

Phase Four
Procrastination and laziness

This is one I have struggled with the most lately and admit it has been one of my biggest hurdles in general. I will refer to an example from a great book a recently read called the war or art by Steven Pressfield which I highly recommend you read. In this book he talks about resistance as the basic enemy in which holds anyone back from doing their work, now we feel this force through different forms, one of which is procrastination or that mischievous imp inside of us that hits a wall and wants to waste time instead of working on ourselves and our issues. One thing I have noticed is this resistance is greater on some days than others. I can wake up one morning early beaming with enthusiasm and want to complete all the day's tasks and have a deep sense of satisfaction doing it. Otherwise, I wake up and go "no... not today" I don't understand why this is but here's the thing, if I feel like this and force myself through it and still set out and do the things I want or know I need to do, I feel even better at the end of the day. This is because I've overcome a large mental hurdle in which I never thought I would be able to overcome. I am sure you have had days like this too, we all have. Unfortunately, though it doesn't always work out like that, sometimes I listen to that very persuasive imp and veg out all day. Let me tell you these are the worst days by far, not only do I feel less accomplished as a result but physically and mentally I feel pretty crappy and am more prone to argue with my family and neglect eating a healthy meal or engage in my daily jog. The best way I've been able to counteract this is to visualize or do a short meditation session in which I think about how this will affect me on multiple levels later, how it will affect those around me and what the consequences of procrastination will entail regarding productivity. Sometimes simply not knowing what to do next can be a trigger for procrastination, in which case obsession can kick in, and compulsive behaviour to over-clean and over-organize my surroundings. What I have found to be particularly helpful in these situations is to quiet the mind through meditation, doesn't matter which type you do just letting yourself be and not judging any thought that may enter your mind, meditate and see where your body and mind naturally take you. This practice is best achieved when done on a consistent basis. As an exercise make a journal just for one week and catalogue your accomplishments for that week and try to determine which days you tend to accomplish more (I recommend an app called daily mood as this allows you to easily rate your overall mood for that day and write a comment about what may have triggered that mood). Also, write down how you feel on each day, just in general and how you reacted to those feelings through what work you have accomplished, most importantly how you felt after accomplishing your work. Try to find any patterns as to what's affecting your levels of motivation for specific days.

There's a fire burning in my eyes

Even the impossible can be done
because I believe it can
the toughest challenge can be won
because I am a fighting man
...there's a fire burning in my eyes,
because I'm after the prize.

Anything far-fetched can be achieved
yes, it can be done

> *because in truth I believe*
> *that I am the right one*
> *but that's no surprize,*
> *cause' there's a fire burning in my eyes.*
>
> *Anything unlikely can be overcome*
> *in an hour of darkness*
> *even though there exists some*
> *who think the situation is hopeless*
> *but my spirit never dies,*
> *because there's a fire burning in my eyes.*
>
> *My heart is ablaze*
> *with the flame of triumph*
> *my soul alight*
> *with this fire of success*
> *an eternal inferno*
> *rages within me*
> *and when you peer into my eyes*
> *then you will see*
> *the fire burning within.*
>
> *...The fire burning within my eyes.*

This chapter has explored the art of persistence and why it's so important to find motivation every single day, even when you are not motivated. There are many triggers for procrastination, and it's fundamental to locate these triggers and take steps in eliminating them. Persistence and staying motivated go hand in hand like two accomplished tango dancers and is what we will concentrate on developing as a first step. If you can create a positive routine of good habits, you will soon find you will naturally flush out the counter-productive ones. The first task is simple, choose a productive task that you know you should do, such as keeping the kitchen clean for three days in a row, once you can accomplish that aim for six days, then 12, etc until you have established consistency. This is very important in retraining your brain into more positive habits and is what scientists refer to as Neuro-Linguistic Programming or NLP and has been proven by countless studies to reshape our brains physically and create more helpful thought patterns and habit building behaviors. As it's been said before you don't want to try and stop the bad habits, you want to replace them with good ones; this will prove much more successful long term. Let's now have a look at the right motivators, but first this week's challenge.

Challenge yourself: It's time for our end of chapter challenge! For this challenge set yourself one goal, does not matter what it is or how big or small, just something you're not currently doing.

Write it down either on paper or in your phone and set it as your background image (Temporarily). Now write a time underneath that goal that you will dedicate every day to striving towards, even if it's just 5 to 10 minutes. For the next 4 weeks following this goal every day at the designated time you have set. If you can't do it at that time on a certain day for any reason, make sure you still find the time that day to do it.

This is going to be a persistence and habit building exercise to start motivating you in one area, for each day you complete your goal or progress toward your goad, place a tick on a calendar to signify its completion. After every week of ticking off your progress everyday reward yourself with something, you love whether it be going out for a nice meal, buying a nice item of clothing, or just chilling our listening to music for an hour. This is important as it will prime your brain to crave rewards as a result of working towards your goals, and as this

skill grows it will help you to achieve other, larger goals. If you can start small and work your way up and you will likely find as you create one useful habit, you start forming other beneficial habits that complement the original.

Chapter 2

The right motivators

Remember,
Your dreams
Are as hungry
As your demons
Make sure
You're feeding the
Right ones
Kushandwizdom

In chapter one, we explored persistence, and why it is so important in staying motivated, now we will dig deep as to why we want to stay persistent with the 'right motivators.'

Success is 90% why and 10% how. I'm not sure if someone has said this before, but to me, it is true. Think about it. When was the last time you wanted something so bad that you would try literally just about anything to get it? it was almost like "the how" didn't matter, you were so determined to get that gold nugget of your eye that you would explore every way of obtaining it because you just HAD to have it. The why is the independent variable because it doesn't matter how you get it as long as you do. It is like the king in a chess game that must be protected at all costs while "the how's" are numerous pawns that can be sacrificed to save the king. The why dictates everything because it is what gives our lives meaning in the end and adds value to our existence. Say for instance you want to save the environment just for the sake of doing something, there is no drive behind it or emotional attachment to the cause, if you want to save the environment to ensure the wellbeing of your future generations so they can have a better tomorrow than we do, that's a powerful "why". Once the motivating factor is rooted in your heart, it naturally tends to find out many "how's" on how to achieve that purpose. Every aspect of your life then becomes part of that decision, and multiple avenues reveal themselves as the light on in the hallway that illuminates the adjacent rooms. Whatever your cause or vision, how do you feel about it? Does it truly inspire you? Is it always on your mind? Is it so strongly a part of you that losing it is the equivalent of losing yourself? These are the questions that will help you find your "why", your motivating factor. Before I do anything anymore, I ask myself, why do I want to do this? What difference will it make if I don't do it? How important is this to me? Don't worry about what anyone else says. If you know in your heart you want to do something, you go after it with everything you've got. Life is too short to accept mediocrity as just 'part of your being', life is meant to be an amazing experience, so always find your biggest why and let the how's flow to you!

The overnight millionaire

Now this is an interesting one, I'm sure most of us have heard of someone really lucky who's won the lottery or come into a substantial fortune by some means, the news comes on that night and proclaims it " such and such from some Town has won 27 million dollars in tonight's power ball," we all get jealous and say things like "I deserve that money or that should have been me, or you lucky bastards" then we go about our lives and then hear three weeks later that the husband who claimed the ticked divorced the wife and tried to run away with the money, or hosted a five million dollar party with a bunch of hookers and strangers and then turned to drugs, alcohol, fancy cars and inevitably… 'bankruptcy'. This doesn't always happen, but I have heard many instances of the sort. The fact is there was no discipline in the acquisition of that fortune, so the winner has gone from a mindset of survival ("They may have been just getting by") to invincible ("I can now have whatever I want") all in but an instant. It's a shock to the system with no surge protection. The overnight millionaire scarcely is ever truly successful for this reason, there is usually a very poor "why" behind its summoning, why's such as "I just want to quit my job and retire so I can enjoy the good life in luxury" or "yay, I can finally afford that Audi R8 I've been fantasising about since last year". This kind of "why" does not represent true motivational power and does not lead to any real or lasting sense of purpose. It only serves as an avenue for our egos and primitive urges to satisfy themselves, and once they have had their fill, they just come crying back for more the next day. This is why most instant millionaires of the sort inevitably fall back into the scarce situation in which they were trying to find a quick escape from. A "why" that was too weak to form true wealth and lasting change. Learn from such examples and become wiser in yourself.

Now, on the other hand, the most successful people I've ever heard of first found their true "why" in life then sought out how they were going to achieve their burning desires and visions for a better tomorrow. They gained the skills and discipline needed to enhance their visions and promote it, perfect it and share it. A lot of them are not even what we might think of as noble or secularly educated to an overtly high degree, but still they have changed our lives for the better, and as a result, they enjoy prosperity for it, companies like Microsoft, Apple, Facebook, eBay, Amazon and a whole lot more. They all started with a strong 'why' for what they went after, then because they invested in that 'why', many how's revealed themselves and were capitalised on and success became a natural by-product for their outcomes.

Where does your motivation stem from?

What I mean by this is, does your motivation stem from your emotional side or your intellectual side? It is a simple question but answers a lot. We are hard-wired to be emotional beings, we feel joy, sadness, fear, regret, mercy, shame, excitement, anger, and other emotions, this you already know but what is interesting is that emotions elicit actions and motivation, we feel fear, so we fight or flee, we feel hungry, so we eat, we feel sad, so we cry. We link emotion to meaning and meaning to tasks, visions, goals, dreams, events, and a multitude of situations throughout life. Say a young boy witnesses a fire growing up, say he had seen the negative effects of that fire and the damage to lives and families it caused for him, this likely has an emotional impact on the boy. He feels a deep sense of sorrow for the lives of the family it has crippled. He feels so strongly about it that his passion is to become a fireman and help prevent or minimise fires in his community, so he naturally from those emotions feels motivated to become the best darn fireman in the country so he can save lives and minimalize potential disasters in the future.

Now say we flip the coin though and look to a child with an incredibly high IQ, a child of virtually limitless capabilities, sure they have what It takes to accomplish anything but why do they feel compelled to do it? Is it going to satisfy them in some way or cater to an emotional deficiency? The reason we do anything in life is to feel a certain way; we want to feel good inside. We eat chocolate because it tastes good, we work out because it helps us look good, and that in turn makes us feel good, we play certain games because it's fun, we listen to music because it evokes positive emotions in us that we want to experience. So, when you ask yourself the question, why do I want to stay motivated, you know it's because ultimately you want to continue to feel good and experience pleasure on a consistent basis, the pleasure you get from finding and living that in which gives your life the most meaning.

The pleasure in pain

What do I mean by this? Quite simply a lot of things we do cause short term pain, things such as exercising for 30 minutes 5 times a week (if you do), doing the dishes every night after dinner, going to work, meeting the dreaded in-laws. These are often painful to do physically and emotionally so why do they in the first place? Simply, because we know that if we keep doing them, if we stay motivated long enough, we will see the fruits of our hard work and persistence through positive relationships both in ourselves and in our environments. Sometimes enduring short-term pain can result in long term pleasure in cases like exercise for example and keeping a regular healthy eating schedule, the same is true in reverse too. If you are constantly seeking instant gratification through binge eating/drinking, gambling, pornography, obsessive television watching, gaming or any other means you are in fact telling yourself you can't function without these vices in your life. Soon you will grow dependant on them for their dopamine-releasing effects. Hence addiction is born, and of course, you know the nature of addiction, soon you need more and more of the same thing to gain the same amount of pleasure from it.

Nine times out of ten you are going to be unmotivated in achieving your goals. That is a fact of life and it is almost without a doubt going to be a struggle, but once the ball is rolling and you force yourself to start and break through that pain, the easier it gets.

The right people to motivate you

Just as we need the right motivators to get us motivated, the kind of people we choose to associate with plays a huge role in our ability to stay motivated. Say you want to eat and maintain a healthy diet, but on the other hand, you have your so-called best friend there with you who wants to go to McDonalds 30 times a week and binge on cheeseburgers, fries, and desserts. Now every weekend at lunchtime you have the choice to spend half an hour preparing a nice Greek salad or take a quick drive to get a large Big Mac meal with a side of nuggets. This would be much quicker and will probably taste a lot better, won't it? Say you are strong enough to turn it down today; will you be strong enough next weekend? How about the weekend after that? You see, it starts wearing down at your will power and every time you're munching on your healthy salad, your friend here brings the aroma of Big Mac sauce and fries straight to your nose. Once your senses start attuning themselves to the McDonalds aroma time after time, subconsciously, your brain sends you triggers to crave that and act on those ever-increasing cravings. This makes achieving your goals that much harder and when you are trying to stay motivated you need the kind of people in your life who will support whatever goals you have and either respect them or be somewhere else when they know they will have a negative effect on you. Choose your associates wisely because they have a much larger impact than you think they do.

> *"Bad associations spoil useful habits"*
> 1 Corinthians 13:33

Are you with someone who doesn't give a damn about your goals? Let me tell you that 9 times out of 10, the changes never happen. Many people go into a relationship under the assumption they can change or fix a person; However, this is hardly the case, instead of fixing a person with lazy and un-motivated ideals the reverse generally happens, as in you pick up their lazy habits and instead of fixing that person, you instead, destroy yourself, unless of course you notice this in time and walk the other way. The kind of people you want to be around are those who build on your motivation and push you to further heights, the kind of people that make you want to challenge yourself every day and be a better you. Sometimes these people are hard to find but at the end of the day you will know when you have found such a person, for your life will actually feel like a forward movement with ease rather than a struggle against the tide.

The right routine to motivate you

Staying motivated in achieving any goal starts first thing in the morning when you wake up from the sweetness of a sound good night's sleep, from the very moment you stammer or leap out of bed and decide what your time is worth to you. Therefore, also your routine the night before. Your first step in establishing a positive routine is having a good night sleep and being consistent in your bedtime and waking up times. It's very hard to stay motivated at any task when you're tired all day and can't concentrate on simple tasks yet alone move closer to your ultimate goals. Before deciding what time to go to bed at night, first figure out what time you want/need to wake up to start, not everyone needs a full 8 hours of sleep but somewhere around that figure is the consensus. The best way to test this is to choose a time when you have a few days off and keep the same wake-up time but alter what times you wind down and go to bed by 30 minutes to find out when you feel most refreshed. This is because everyone's circadian rhythm is different, each cycle of sleep generally lasts around 90 minutes, and restful sleep that refreshes you is apparent when you wake up naturally at the end of a completed cycle. This means it doesn't matter if you get 8 or more hours of sleep in the night, if you wake up in the middle of a cycle, you will likely feel drowsy for several hours. This is also why it's best to wake up naturally without the aid of an alarm clock and only use one as a backup if needed. Remember, your daily routine starts when you wake up and is affected by the quality of your sleep. Starting your day rested and energised is the first key deposit in your bank of daily motivation.

Only you can decide what a good morning routine is to you. If you do wake up rested and full of energy its best to start knocking items off your to-do list straight away. Your daily allotment of willpower starts depleting the moment you get up so as a general rule you want to start doing the largest and most challenging tasks first. If you have a large number of tasks to complete it may be better to start instead by eliminating the smaller ones quickly, so you don't overwhelm yourself later on. Remember also to have a small break between tasks to refresh yourself and think about the next task(s) on your list. It is also wise to spread tasks out over the week, so you're not doing everything in one day and then struggling to find things the next day, by doing this it is much easy to stay motivated consistently rather than in the occasional large burst of motivation.

Once you have successfully tackled and tamed your morning routine it's time to move on with the rest of the day. It's amazing to get a great start for the day but that is still only a portion of the battle, once you have the momentum of a successful morning it's time to push that motivation ball and keep it going for the rest of the day!

Breaking the identity barrier

What you have is not who you are. I would highly encourage you to read a book called Minimalism by Joshua Fields Millburn & Ryan Nicodemus. In their journeys they discuss how they both earned a 6-figure income and were basically set for life in their respective careers, one was even offered the position of junior partner with his firm, however, his reaction to this offer was to go back to his office, lock the door, and weep in his chair. The reason being was that he felt stuck in a rut, if he accepted, he would not be able to just up and leave on a whim, it would effectively mean he was locked in for life. Knowing that this was his only life to live, he declined and left the firm, sold all of his useless junk and adopted the minimalist lifestyle.

The lesson is that possessions are only there to fill a void in our lives, a void in which things replace meaningful interactions and life experiences. Affluence does not define who we are but rather, holds us back from the things that truly matter — Think of your time on this planet as a large sack that you carry around behind you. The more you accumulate, the harder it becomes to walk and move forward, and eventually, it becomes too heavy, and you become paralysed by the sheer weight of useless possessions. Too much 'stuff' saps us of joy and energy, and drains us with the false belief that, "It's all about who can collect the most toys" which by the way, rot, rust, and lose value over time. Breaking the identity barrier by minimalizing what we have and the useless things we do (Like watch too much television and engage in pointless arguments about unimportant and valueless activities for example) we gain an unprecedented level of motivation, energy, and clarity in what matters most to us as individuals in a world of increasing distractions. Simplify your life, maximise your energy!

Perfectionism and its destructive ideals

The trait of perfectionism is a loaded firearm to the head in staying motivated. Granted, doing a job well is aptly warranted, but the preoccupation with having something perfect is not only unrealistic, but also not a healthy quality to have for your sanity. For one thing, perfection is an unreachable ideal in this world, nothing is perfect, and the universe can be thought of as 'organised chaos' that operates under the order of 'difference and variety are an expression of beauty' that makes life so interesting. Imperfections, in essence, create uniqueness. Another flaw with perfection can be thought of as an exponential graph where you have a horizontal asymptote. This is the curved line that keeps approaching the x-axis but never touches it. Perfectionism is like that asymptote, we can strive and strive all we want to get there, we will get closer and closer, but never actually attain that standard, instead, we will just end up wasting countless time and effort in pursuit of something illusory and where the degree of time spent on that standard starts to create diminishing returns, and that is how you drain your valuable energy and motivation with the velocity of a piercing bullet. On the other hand, it's a great thing to strive for excellence in all you do, but it only becomes a problem when you refuse to stop because you feel it's just never good enough. The antidote for perfectionism is realism and acceptance of your uniqueness, you were made to be you with all your quirks and traits, warts and moles, and scars of experience, so you can share with the world your unique angle on life and art in a way that only you can and ever will. Remember that nothing is perfect, and that's perfectly okay!

Realism vs. Perfectionism

Does realism mean you should accept whatever circumstance and learn to live with it? By no means. Being realistic is akin to a trained skill, one that I've personally needed to work on throughout my life. According to one study, 92% of people who fail to achieve their goals are because they set them too unrealistically. Most people go from 0 to 100, not realising that its best to start with manageable goals first and work your way up to more challenging goals, just as you would if you were lifting weights at the gym, start small and gradually increase either the weight, reps, or sets to increase your gains gradually. This is realism, it's that simple, start small and finish big, want to run 10km a day, start with 1km a day, then work your way up to 2km a day, then 3km and so on. The reason why people do this? Impatience, wanting results now. Therefore, two muscles need to be worked on, 1: Patience, and 2: Realism. How do you work on these? Once again by starting small, setting small achievable expectations in both these areas, and working up to bigger targets.

Learn to ignore the BS

That's right, learning to ignore negative belief systems, whether they be self-conjured or cast at you by others. Negative belief systems whether obvious or subconscious have a profound impact on our ability to stick something out or give up at the first sign of resistance.

Granted, it is challenging if someone is yelling negativity straight into your eardrum, yet the way we react is going to determine the entirety of our outcome. If you are strong enough to laugh off a brash remark, then you are already miles ahead of the pack. Learning to ignore negativity is another invaluable skill, one that does take practice but once mastered will be a lifelong trait. Not taking people or events personally is perhaps the most efficient way to recover from any blow that life deals to you. This is what some may call 'grit' or 'resilience' and is a quality that a lot of centenarians swear by as a key way to stay healthy and young longer than those who can't be bothered to attain it. Negativity, however, is not just an external phenomenon that invades us through the harsh criticisms of others, it is primarily a self-taught and self-inflicted bullet wound from the gun known as 'The untrained mind', and language is all too often the trigger the empties the chamber. From birth on, we learn toxic phrases like, "I Can't", "It's impossible", or "I am not good enough". Phrases like this do more than tear your motivation down, they affect you on a cellular level, to the point where your physical body starts to believe you and act by your harsh demands. Eliminate such phrases from your vocabulary and oust them into the flames of yesterday, instead start empowering yourself with phrases that bolster your defence against the vicious onslaught of negativity that will test your resolve every day! Phrases like "I Can", "I am worth of it" and "I will do it" will serve to boost you with the necessary grit to move forwards every day.

A.L.M

Accept it, learn from it, and Move forward

This is a phrase that I have only recently adopted, but I make sure every single day that I am doing my best to apply it. I, like many others have at one time or if not most of the time have been confronted with a problem of some kind and just complained about it. A.L.M is the basic formula for confronting any situation; 1 – Accept that you have a problem and don't live in denial about it. 2 – Learn from the problem, whether it's an issue that you caused or that happened as a result of the environment or situation that you put yourself into, learn what caused it or how you can better deal with it next time, or better yet, not repeat the issue or repeat putting yourself in the situation in which the issue occurred. 3 – Move forward. Complaining about the situation is the classic trait of a lazy, weak minded person who knows there is a problem and knows something needs to be done but can't be bothered finding a workable solution or doesn't want to put in the work required to solve it. These three steps are a great way to establish the right mindset to tackle any issue and come out stronger, wiser and with a more realistic attitude afterwards.

Compare yourself only to yourself

If you continue to compare
Yourself to others you will become bitter.
If you continue to compare
Yourself with yourself, you will become
Better.
-Unknown-

I am not exactly clear on who wrote these words of wisdom, but there is such truth and gold in them. One of the greatest issues in society today is we've grown into such a competitive species that people can become violent and antisocial when desires are not met. Sport is a great example of just how competitive we've become. Many riots have been the result of crazed sports fans giving in to their animal instincts when their favourite team either wins or loses, 12 people were killed in Harare, Zimbabwe in 2000 as the result of enraged fans rioting during a world cup qualifier. With the massive growth in the fashion industry and fashion magazines, the standard of physical beauty in today's culture has become so high that most people feel they cannot reach such standards of beauty. They compare themselves to supermodels and end up spending thousands of dollars on cosmetics in order to become like their aspired heroes. This is the basic goal of the fashion industry in the first place, to make you feel 'inadequate' with who you are and as a result, buy their lavish products, so you become someone that you're not. The fact is these trends promote the wrong kind of motivation, they in effect tell you that you are not good enough on your own devices, then taunt you with images of models covered in half their body weight of make-up, special effects and expensive lighting. Motivation works very powerfully in this way, it manifests most when we are feeling low, thinking others have it better, then creating a desire strong enough to merit change, generally the greater the pain, the greater the feelings of motivation to improve. This is why it is so dangerous to compare yourself to others, it only breeds pain, bitterness, and jealousy. Only focus on comparing yourself to how you were yesterday, that way you can really measure your degree of improvement and become better consistently!

WORK ON YOUR INNER DEMONS, NOT THAT OF OTHERS

*"When there is
no enemy within,
the enemies outside
cannot hurt you."
African Proverb*

When confronted with conflict from others, it is normal for us to want to convince ourselves that the other party is wrong and that in some way we should turn them over to our way of doing or thinking things. This is basic human behaviour at a primitive level that we instinctively possess. However, it is important to be cognizant of when this takes place as it can not only lead to greater conflicts but also greatly impair our existing and potential relationships. The only thing that we have a true sense of control over is ourselves, and zero control of anyone else, therefore by way of logic it makes sense that if you want something to change you must start with yourself. Conflicts usually arise when there is some kind of miscommunication between parties that become flared when a nerve is struck through an insensitive remark or brash statement. These insecurities that we each possess act as our greatest enemies; these are the real culprits as they reveal innate flaws and shortcomings in our character. It is therefore vital to weed these out by being constantly self-aware and checking how you feel whenever you enter a new situation or a changing one.

If you find yourself getting worked up in certain settings such as the local supermarket or when you're on the freeway, for example, this may signify you have an issue with patience. It would thereby stand to reason that you either start working on that or seek professional help from a psychologist to gain the necessary skills to improve in this area. When your internal issues are under control and well maintained it is much easier to remain resilient under stressful circumstances. In effect, things generally don't bother us as much; I am sure you have experienced times when this has proven true. Remember, when confronted with any form of conflict, reflect on why you felt the way you did and what caused you to react in the way you did so you can better understand your triggers and qualities you need to work on. By being the best version of you, you will be building an inner peace that is almost unbreakable, so start working on yourself.

Challenge Yourself: This week's challenge is about finding the right motivators for you, this will involve a bit of self-searching, but it will be of great help both in the short and long term. For this, you will need someone who you can rely on such as

a close friend or family member. You will need a specific goal that you have either been working on or plan to start soon, you will tell this person your goal, and you will describe it to them in every detail, you will map out to them why you want to achieve this goal so badly and what steps you plan on taking to finish it. Most importantly you are going to give yourself a reasonable time limit to finish it. Once you have told this goal to your selected person, you will ask them to report back on you every week, preferably at the end of each week. You will set an alarm reminder on your phone every week also at the end of each week that will prompt you to check and evaluate your progress for that week. You will need to be honest with yourself here as the degree of your goals success will depend on it. If you are successful in achieving your allotment for that week, you will reward yourself with something you greatly enjoy; ideally this reward will be slightly different each week to keep it fun, but it can be the same. If you fail to achieve what you set out to achieve, don't beat yourself up, no one's perfect, However, you will need to write down why you didn't complete your goal for that week and find the issue (was it time constraints, lack of energy, laziness etc.) only you will really know why you did not achieve it, then you will need to write down what you plan to do to change that next week. Again, it is important that you choose someone responsible here who can support and encourage you through this as this will likely be important to you, tell them to be harsh with you and not sugar-coat your lack of progress. Remember too, you are looking for the right motivators, so you also want to keep track of the things you are allowing into your minds such as TV programmes, music, associations and even your self-talk, so journal as much as you can. I know this is a lot, but at the end of the day, the best investment you can have it in yourself, so invest your time wisely.

Chapter 3

Keeping your eyes on the prize

*The clearer you are
when visualising your dreams,
the brighter the spotlight
will be to lead you
on the right path.*
Gail Lynne Goodwin

From where does motivation extend? Why do we need motivation and to stay motivated anyway? The desire to have something gives birth to motivation, hence why it is so important to know what you want out of life. If you rarely feel motivated anymore, don't fret, most of us live the life of the wheel-bound hamster, running in an endless circle getting nowhere and getting good at it, building the muscle of least resistance and laziness until it is a front-liner at a Mr Universe contest? This represents the life of the person hoping that if they run around in the same circle long enough, something will become of it, something magical that just manifests itself and waves its wand over your existence and somehow radically change you into the prince of drive and motivation. Realistically, only when someone falls off that wheel and chooses to take a different path do things start to happen for that person, they take complete responsibility for their own lives and decisions and realize they themselves are fully accountable for everything they have in their lives and in themselves. Once they have fallen off that wheel this person knows what he no longer wants or is willing to accept and he is thus one step closer to where he wants to be by a process of hard-learned elimination.

IT MUST BE WHAT YOU WANT!

I've asked more than a dozen people what they want to do with their lives, and every answer was invariably the same, "I don't know" or "I haven't given it much thought" to be honest I haven't asked myself that question enough in my own life. The desire to want something generally stems from our own experience and therefore in someone becomes a product of trial and error, how does a professional bowler know that is his dream if he has never seen, tried, or heard of bowling before? The fact is he doesn't, so the only way we will ever find out what we are passionate about is if we experience new things in our lives regularly enough and commit to having an open mind about them. When we are young and highly impressionable, we tend to want validation from our parents, and they usually have ideals for us, you should become a lawyer or a doctor, or x career that pays y dollars, and as kids what we want is to fulfil their expectations of us as they are our sole influence in life.

As we grow into our teenage years our time becomes divided between our parents and now, our new peers, we then gleam new insights and ways of thinking from them. We start liking the same music and ideals as them and our wants then change again. After a while we graduate school and enter corporate society which again has a much different ideal to our former ones, you must dedicate all your time and passion into your new job. It's no wonder people don't know what they want out of life; different ideals bombard us on an ever-changing basis. Our biology changes and so does our desires, subtly but surely. True dreams, true desires, true passions never do, they scream out to us in the beginning, hoping we will hear, and a few of us do early on, most of us though only casually listen like a kid pretending to listen to his mother whilst trying to defeat that level he has been stuck on in his video game for weeks. Once we ignore that voice long enough it loses its energy and grows quieter like the fading sun over the ocean that precedes night. Eventually, we can no longer hear that voice of urgency and all that's left is the acceptance of your current circumstances. This is one of the saddest things in life to me, and my goal is to stop it or at least make it easier to see.

WE MUST QUIET DOWN ALL THOUGHT TO TRULY LISTEN

The only way we can reclaim this voice is by becoming truly silent and completely still, what do I mean by this? When you want to hear someone talk at a noisy party, what you do? turn the music down of course, we each have so many pointless thoughts running through our head every day that it's hard to separate the wheat from the chaff. You need to get away from all that, even for just a few minutes and just be in the moment. Feel your surroundings and let your inner voice be heard again; deep down you know what you need to do. All you need is to take the first step and silence your mind truly, meditate, speak honestly with yourself and do what you know you must do. Step away from your pointless thoughts and routines for just a day and you will hear clearly what your mind is trying to tell you.

KEEP A MENTAL AND PHYSICAL PICTURE OF WHAT YOU WANT EVERYWHERE YOU GO

If you want something badly enough, you will find a way to get it, end of story, that's it. Find out what you want and damn well do what you must do to get it, if an obstacle gets in the way, either move the obstacle or find a way around it, if people turn against you, too bad! It just wasn't meant to be. In life, there are always going to be stumbling blocks, naysayers, false friends, and people turning their backs on you, shortcomings, disasters, unforeseen events, hesitation, and doubts. Guess what, Beethoven had them, Einstein had them, Michael Jordan had them, Oprah and every single other person who has remained motivated to live their dreams had them. You are not the only one with them so stop making them your excuse to accept mediocrity. Get out there and make it happen, and if you don't know what you want yet, find it by trying as many different things as possible until you find your resonance, it is NEVER too late, no matter what anyone says, so make every moment count for YOUR own sake.

I highlighted above that you absolutely should keep both a mental AND a physical picture of what you want with you at all times, this cannot be emphasised enough, if you want the double story house at the end of the street then carry the best picture of it with you all the time, if you want that spectacular beach body, carry around a picture of someone with that body already, if you want more money, literally carry around a picture of a large wad of cash with you in your wallet, so every time you look at it you get that awesome feeling of what it would be like to have enough money to do whatever you want in life. These are powerful subtle psychological tools that will prime you into constantly focusing on what you DO want rather than just fantasise about it and never act. The more of that energy you put out there the more of it will come back to you, the more it will shape your attitude and behaviour to stay motivated enough to go after it no matter what is thrown your way.

Concrete imagery

*Concreteness transports us
into a story like nothing else.
It's the key that unlocks the door
Of the reader's imagination.
Kim Kautzer.*

Images of your goals, dreams, and desires must be vivid, specific, and serve as constant reminders of your vision. It is not enough to simply imagine your goals and think about them from time to time; they must consistently be Concrete in your mind! This is why you should carry a physical image of what you want to achieve with you, so when you are that busy and don't think about it for some time, you have a reminder there to put you back on track.

I don't use the word positive imagery here, I use the word concrete for good reason, firstly we all have many thousands of thoughts on a daily basis, most of them forgotten very quickly, especially neutral and positive thoughts. Negative thoughts though tend to want to outstay their welcome and linger for sometimes hours, days, or weeks on end. Concrete thoughts also have this innate survivability in that they can stick around for much longer periods of time, this is why you want to solidify positive imagery into your mind, how do you do this? Start and End each and every day by not only actively imagining your goal, but also imagine the process of working up to it and actually finishing it, feel it within yourself with each breath you take. Feel the joy and tingles you get when that goal is a tangible realisation to you. Again, keep a physical image or even images of that dream and how it will look to you on your bed stand so first thing you see when you wake up is your dream and the last thing you see before you go to bed is that dream enforced upon your visual mind once again. We retain most of what we learn when we wake up in the morning and it is strengthened if we focused on it before we slept the previous night, this is exactly why I stress the importance of this habit, it really can and will change your life if you apply it. Let me stress too that this is a 'habit', so you will experience increasingly positive results the more consistently you practice this routine. Remember to not just think positively about your goal but to make the image of it concrete by instilling its vivid physical image of its completion in your mind first thing when waking up in the morning and last thing before going to bed, this will help you keep your eyes on the prize of your goals and stay motivated to finish them.

Carry the visual image of what you want every day. Carry a physical reminder of it with you to look at for inspiration. Imagine vividly and profoundly what it would be like to hold that specific dream in your hand, feel it, smell it, taste it. Imagine vividly and profoundly how you will feel when you finally hold that realization in your eager palms. Never settle for anything less and believe 100% that it is already yours, this will motivate you beyond words and drill into your subconscious mind the passion you have for your dream, and naturally, you will start to see the steps you need to take to start making it a realization.

The purpose of the obstacles

Obstacles
Are designed
To make you
Stronger,
Only the weak
Avoid them.
PictureQuotes.com

Many, if not all of us despise obstacles; you know the pesky little nonsense that gets between you and success. I can understand this too, they are frustrating to say the least, but also highly necessary. You see obstacles are there to test you, sometimes a little more than you like, but they serve to test you to see if what you're going after is indeed what you actually want or if it's just some phantom belief in your head of what you think you want. As humans we change and constantly grow so it's no wanders our natural rhythms change too, sometimes our brains tell us they want this, other times something different, it's unpredictable, to say the least. So, if for some bizarre reason you find yourself wanting something in life, doesn't matter what, you will be tested!

The sands of time test all, reveal all, and never lie. If we are finding ourselves quickly cracking under pressure and giving up quickly, chances are, you didn't want it that badly anyway. Embrace obstacles and let them refine your goals and reveal within yourself what you truly desire, this will help you to stay motivated in going after what you really want.

Can you force yourself to be motivated most of the time?

Motivation seems to follow a cycle, a subtle one. Seems like half the days I get out of bed and I just feel it, the other half… let's not even go there. Is there an explanation for this? Is there a way to overcome it? Motivation is fleeting and unpredictable, sometimes it's just there, other times it seems to be on a 3-week vacation in Hawaii and may not want to return. From the years of personal observation and research, the only constant I have noticed as to what affects my motivation levels is rather simple. I suffer from OCD (obsessive compulsive disorder) so generally my mind races throughout the day and hardly ceases at night. This constant thinking leads me to question a lot of things and focus of mundane thoughts and thinking styles. Generally, I know what I want but then I notice something else and wander if that might be a better option, so I investigate it and develop an interest in it, and so on and so forth, to the point that at many times in my life I have been plagued and paralysed by indecision. Be very careful of this as especially in this day and age, we have almost endless possibilities available to us and basically if we want something we can have it almost instantaneously. This kind of mindset of going from one thing to the next is a motivation killer! Have you ever noticed on TV during an ad break there will be an ad for say, McDonald's, then straight after it's finished a Subway commercial then 2 ads after that KFC? Suddenly, we are confronted with 3 mouth-watering options in which we want all of them but end up with none because it was too difficult to choose. In essence staying motivated should never become a to-do list of many things compounding your time, it requires complete focus in specific goals that you are actually passionate about. This step can take time, especially if like most people you don't know what you really want or where to start, many times in life you just have to try new things to see what sparks an interest, there is no grey area here, you will know if you really enjoy something as opposed to if you don't enjoy it and you have to give it a fair go as well as your best effort. Another killer of motivation and drive occurs when your goals don't line up with your values, it's something easy to miss but sometimes hard to notice why. This is another reason why it's so important to silence the mind at the end of each day, so you can hear your own voice in the absence of all the distractions that occur in today's world.

Focus, focus, focus really is the key here, don't spread yourself out to thinly as one wise counsellor told me, focus on one thing at a time, period! Devote all of your energy to its full completion and then move on, If you don't know how to prioritize your goals then think of it this way, say you have a machine that manufactures various parts in a warehouse, then say this machine has some faulty wiring and needs fixing and it starts affecting its production efficiency of the parts it must manufacture, the manager must choose between repairing the machine or increasing its run speed by ramping up the manufacture line speed and hiring more labour, you have a limited budget so you can only fix one of these issues, which one do you choose? Think of your body as that machine and your goals as the parts you are producing for your production line, sure you can ramp up the speed of the factory to try and do more to compensate for the machines slow-down, but this means getting additional staff, not only that but the more you work the overworked machine, the more maintenance it needs and the slower it gets resulting in more labour needing to be hired. Or you can solve the root cause of the issue; fix the machine first so it can accomplish its tasks without the need for speed-up, thus resulting in greater efficiency of production. Clearly fixing the machine is a better option; likewise, if you have a personal problem or need to work on your health first, then you should start there! Your current degree of health will ultimately determine just how much you can accomplish. External goals do not mean anything if we are not well enough or have not the strength to fulfil them so remember to always look after your health first and promptly fix any issues you may have either mentally, emotionally, spiritually, or physically first, once you are at this level you will have all the energy you need to stay motivated to manufacture your desired goal.

Challenge your fears

*Everything
You've ever
Wanted
Is on the
Other side of
Fear.
George Adair*

Every day we are confronted with opportunities to confront our fears and ultimately grow as individuals. Do you know that feeling you get when you do something you're not comfortable with? That feeling of accomplishment! Not only that but doesn't it also motivate you to challenge yourself further and confront more of your fears? This is because it gives us self-confidence. Self-confidence is one of the primal forces that drives us in staying motivated and without it, staying motivated becomes more and more difficult. Even just starting with smaller fears and challenges and working our way up slowly is great for building confidence and hence, staying motivated in achieving our goals. Some of your greatest experiences will likely exist just beyond your comfort zone, Skydiving as an example is a very rational hobby to be fearful of, jumping out of a plane that is soaring 10,000 feet in the air should frighten most people hence why many would rather watch the Sunday football game, ask though, the people who have conquered this fear and they will likely tell you it's one of the best experiences they've ever had. They will likely tell you too that the hardest part was walking up to the open door on the plane as one of the scariest moments, yet once they took that physical and metaphorical leap of faith and questionability, they felt the greatest surge of exhilaration and adrenaline course through their veins as they soared through the crisp unpopulated air with perhaps the greatest view of their lives. This of course is just one example, but the same is true with tasks such as public speaking or swimming with sharks, there has been many a career change in those who challenges some of their greatest fears because they realized that the fear was only temporary, and they often also realized that what they were in fact afraid of was actually something they loved and were just confusing that fear with the hearts unfulfilled excitement.

There was once a young lad
Who could not lift much
He was thought of as weak
and not manly as such
He would carry along his path
A singe stone
As he trekked through the depths
Of a haunted forest all alone
As time slid by
Surely as the cold winds moaned
He grew stronger and stronger
Carrying that single stone

Before too long
he would gather and amass
every rock and pebble
that he so happened to stumble past
He filled his every pocket
Stone on top of stone
Topping up his bulging backpack
Toiling zone after rugged zone
Soon the young lad
Was a young lad no more
As he ventured back
Tired, bruised and abundantly sore
As he arrived
In a land he knew as home
Not one recognized him
As he carry with him an army of stones
What once was a boy
Of feeble means
Was now a mighty strong man
Strong, sturdy and lean
Challenge yourself every day
And you will become
the warrior you could only dream to be

Remember to work your way up with challenging your fears, starting too large will likely only cause you to retreat back into the shell of comfort that you're so used to. Think of your fears as the steps of a staircase, tackle them from the bottom and one at a time, and try not to be tempted by the urge to be the hurried businessman and skip 3 steps only to trip on the 4th and drop his briefcase of important documents so to speak. most of us though are used to standing on the same step and you will know this because things will start seeming easy and effortless and also not getting to the floor of your goals as it were, being uncomfortable and a bit fearful is a great gauge to let you know that you are well and truly growing as a person and moving from your comfort zone into your goal zone. Whilst consistent growth in fear-challenging is vital for staying motivated it is equally important to have a breather from time to time to relax and celebrate your victories, even your small ones. This will motivate you further to keep conquering your fears. You will in effect start off as a worrier, but the more you fight those fears with your sword of endurance and consistency, you will gradually grow into a mighty warrior who annihilates every obstacle and carries the trophy of their goals.

Keep your eyes fixed directly in front of you, but don't forget to zoom out from time to time.

What is the biggest way for us to lose focus of the finish line? Distraction. These nasty critters can come from all sorts of directions, but the one I want to focus on is the one that lurks behind us, the goal is to look intently and focus on the goal in front of us, when we turn around whilst we are running we don't see the little stumbling blocks we could have avoided if we were paying attention, instead, we fall over, hurt ourselves and then need to recover. The past is great for remembering lessons but to focus on it constantly is like driving on the main road looking in the rear-view mirror, this makes having an accident more a case of when rather than if. One of the biggest hurdles to overcome can often be a past failure or failures that you constantly invite back into your mind; this in effect will lower your motivation and can be likened to slamming your foot on the break whilst looking in the rear-view mirror and yet keep staring in it with a 500-metre gaze.

The best way I have found to avoid this is the focus at the point that is far enough in front of you so you can see impending obstacles but not too far so as to lose sight of what lies right before you, see every goal can be broken down into many sub goals which when combined form our primary goal, much like when you travel a long distance you may stop at a motel to rest for the night and focus and plan on your next course of action. This is why I said don't forget to zoom out sometimes as you want to know where your ultimate destination still is and be constantly reminded of it, but you also want to never lose track of all the small steps that are required to achieve that. Always break your larger goals down into manageable, smaller counterparts that you can work on systematically whilst keeping the bigger picture in mind. Remember, distractions and obstacles are a part of our existence and can rarely be avoided so it's crucial to catch yourself quickly if you find yourself reminiscing on the past or overly focused on the end goal rather than keeping the majority of your focus and energy on the present and the smaller goals that form the larger ones.

Don't give up what you want most, for what you want now
Richard G Scott

Let's talk about something that has become a bigger problem now than it's ever been before…Instant gratification. In a world of quick conveniences and increasingly fast modes of transportation it is easy now to indulge on not only just about anything, but anything that can be held in a matter of minutes, hours or days. Looking back a mere century ago if you wanted to travel overseas you would need an entire season off work to commute via the Pacific or Indian ocean, now you can do it in less than half a day. It is so often taken for granted the availability of today's luxuries that many of us don't give a second thought when making trivial decisions such as should I go through the drive-through? Or let's purchase that second car. Impulse decision-making is at epidemic proportions today with the advertising industry taking full advantage of this by exploiting our weakness of gaining 'the path of least resistance'. Sure, you can prepare a healthy meal but hey, why would you when we can make it for you in under a minute and for 25% less. We are hard-wired to seek comfort and ease so after a tough day at work it's an almost obvious choice to give in, that's why most radio ads are targeted after 5pm when most finish their shifts, that's also why fast food outlets and breweries are strategically placed on the most busy routes home from the industrial sites, they can't catch them all but they will certainly net the weakened ones that have lost their willpower in the present for that 'quick fix'.

This is another reason why you need to keep a vivid image of your short and long-term goals in mind; otherwise, you get distracted in a moment's weakness, lose sight of the obstacle, and stumble into the seductive trap of consumer marketing and constant distraction. This is why I encourage people to keep physical images of their goals in their wallets or nearby at all times, in case of these moments. Remember to always keep in mind what you most desire so you aren't pulled into the trap of instant gratification in order to get what you want in the moment; the short-term pleasure will only cause long term pain when it comes to staying motivated and achieving your ultimate goals.

Challenge Yourself: This week's challenge is going to involve setting up strategic points around your living space and have reminders located at those points. You are going to think about where you spent most of your time around your home and use this to your advantage, first I want you to think about your main long-term goal and describe it to yourself in as much detail as possible, be specific here and don't hold back. Once you have described it to the point where you can basically see it, go onto your web browser, and start screen shotting images of the most relevant to your vision. If you can print them even better. Once you have collected at least one image, but it can be more, then get them printed or have some

sort of hard copies made. Once you have done this you want to place one of these on your fridge, one on your bed stand or somewhere near to your bed, then place them in your most commonly visited areas around the house. This is going to act as a primer for your brain every time you get up and move to a different room or your mood changes. These will become not only conscious reminders but subconscious ones too. The more you look at the physical image of your dream, the more real it's going to become to you and the more motivated you are going to start feeling knowing that no matter where you go, you are reminded of it and you will not be forgetting about it anytime soon, and even when you're not directly thinking about it, subconsciously you will be working it out in your mind.

Chapter 4

Persevere to perspire, working hard at your goals

> *A dream doesn't become reality through magic; it takes sweat, determination and hard work.*
> Colin Powell

How many people have you spoke to in late December telling you how this coming year they are going to achieve all their goals? They say things like "this year I am going to lose 30kg" or "I am going to quit my job and kick-start a new career" etc. New Year's resolutions are great in theory and I do see the benefit of them, however I am yet to meet a single person who has actually fully followed through on their resolute goals. I have never really liked New Year's resolutions to be honest and it's because they create a negative loop in our minds, a sense of delay and withheld expectation. In our minds if we truly want something, right now is the time to start doing it! Not in 3 weeks or 4months or whenever a new year begins. Subconsciously many of us have primed ourselves to wait until the end of the year for a fresh start, it comes, we may start working towards our resolution, and then life gets in the way and throws a curve ball at you, so slowly over time you forget about it. If you have a goal, start doing things to benefit that right now, don't put it off until next year, next month or even next week, start doing things right now even if they are just small steps.

Consistency

Show me the man
Who has mastered a skill
After one attempt,
And I will perhaps show you
A land filled
With flying sheep

This is where we all fall short at times, consistency. This is the most important part of hard work and it is the only part that lets us see the results of that work if we stick it through. Consistency requires disciple and self-sacrifice and is never easy unless you either love what you do or have divine power bestowed upon you. You must prioritise your time to push out all distractions until you have worked on your goals. If you wake up in the morning the first thing you should be working towards is your vision, your will power is a limited resource so therefore use it wisely and as early as possible in the day. Consistency becomes a habit once you have overcome the challenging starting period in which your brain tells you "I have no desire to do this right now" but you must fight against that, at least only for the first 1 to 3 weeks whilst that habit is forming, after that, consistency become like the shoelaces you no longer need to think about to tie. Build your consistency by feeding your routine with the small steps you need to be achieving your larger goals each day, that's right… each day. A good calendar will be your best friend here as if you use it properly it will be able to highlight your actual progress or lack thereof. Like always you need to be honest with yourself here and realize if you are not seeing the results you like, it is all on you! No one else, you must take complete responsibility for your own success or lack of it, only this way will you take responsibility for your own life and not let excuses or laziness get in the way, and if you are successful for the whole week in achieving those small steps then don't hesitate to reward yourself as this will also reinforce the positive application of your new forming habit of consistency. Once consistency is well established motivation will become a by-product for its natural continuation and growth. Remember consistency can often be challenging to maintain but it gets easier the more you practice it, it will eventually become an automatic process, and this is where you want to get to, because at this level you will be constantly improving and moving toward your goals almost without you realizing it.

A little each day is better than a lot at once

*"I don't fear the man
who throws 10,000 punches all at once,
I fear the man
who throws 1 punch 10,000 times"
Bruce Lee.*

Just as the quote states, it's better to do just a little bit every day over a long period of time than try and do everything in one day then forget about it in a weeks' time. Again, this is consistency in action and is vital to the growth and development of any skill, including staying motivated. If you do just one thing a day towards anything, you will soon find that it slips from your conscious mind into your subconscious habits that you do automatically. Don't assume though that this will happen in a fixed amount of time, everyone is different and what takes a month to form a habit for one may take you several, the key is to continue even when you don't feel like it, until it becomes a well-ingrained habit.

Discipline

Discipline is a skill that anyone can build on, it requires discipline to learn the piano, martial arts, or a new language. If these tasks were easy to acquire and could be learned in a day, you would not need discipline to acquire them and their value as a skill would be greatly diminished. Think of disciple as a muscle, the more you exercise it the stronger it gets. The more you overcome the desire to put off goals and procrastinate, the more consistency and self-discipline you develop and the easier it becomes to stay motivated in your pursuits. Someone once said "suffer the pain of discipline or suffer the pain of regret" much like if you don't suffer the pain of exercise and a healthy lifestyle you will suffer the pain of obesity and ailment. Unfortunately, there are a lot of unhappy people in the world who have wasted a lot of time and opportunities through procrastination or just general fear; they look back on their lives with regret and bitterness. The emotional pain it has caused them bears itself in physical manifestations on their hardened faces and hearts; they just look beaten down and defeated, angry and unsatisfied, numb, and lacking purpose or drive. This is a sad and painful reminder of just what a lack of discipline and time wasting can bring upon any of us at any time. Don't let yourself be another statistic of unfulfillment, instead wake up first thing in the morning and get started with your dreams, if you don't feel motivated, them revive that feeling by meditating profoundly on the image of your dream until it energises you. Whatever it takes you must achieve it for yourself and yourself alone!

Plan ahead

Luck favours the prepared! Achieving your goals generally has nothing to do with luck but that's not to say you shouldn't be prepared, really that should be changed to success favours the prepared. Once you have a solid goal in mind you should start to plan how you are going to go about working towards it, one step at a time, try to start small if you can so you don't get overwhelmed too quickly and work your way up to larger steps once you're more comfortable with your progress. Don't just mentally plan your steps, write them down and keep them in eyes view in an area you spend a lot of time generally. Keep a checklist too so you can tick off steps you achieve. These are all simple to do, but don't get complacent as they are also highly effective for not only progress but staying motivated too.

What's just as important as an effective plan and strategy toward your goal is a Timeline and schedule. We all live relatively busy lives so it's vital to plan and prioritise our time effectively. If you don't manage your time, it will manage you and it will constantly provide you with distractions to slow your progress down and even eliminate it. I would highly recommend you read a book called the war of art by Steven Pressfield who teaches us how to overcome this invisible foe known as "resistance" as it offers some very useful tips on annihilating procrastination. Once you have prioritised your time to where it enables you to work on your vision you should set yourself a timeline in which to complete it. If you have a clear time of arrival at your destination of success, it will motivate you further to constantly move ever forward and not waste precious time. A clear timeline will also help you to see if you are on track or if you're falling behind. Your dream should not be like the much-dreaded homework you used to bring home from school and left to the last minute, rather, it should be the thing that you pursue with enthusiasm and excitement because let's face it, your dream is your pass out of mediocrity and into abundance and prosperity!

Do you work till you sweat?

Do you? Only you can honestly answer that question, you know how hard you work towards it or don't work towards it. You know if you are giving it your all or if you can do better. If your goal is to build muscle mass and you do a lot of compound lifts, you know you've had an effective workout because you feel that burn in your muscles and they are physically sore and tired afterward, if you didn't achieve this than you have room for improvement. If your goals are physical in nature you should be exhausted and sweating by the time you finish for the day, if your goals are mentally focused then you should be mentally tired and almost unable to think at the end of the day, this is how the best become the best, by putting in more effort and time in then the competition, if you want the same you must do the same and be the first one in and the last one out when going after your goals.

You are never too busy and overrun to achieve your dream, and if you think you are you need to make time for it and adjust your outlook. Your dream is what makes you different from every other person on this planet and is why you are unique! It's the gift you can give to the world and yourself if you so choose, a gift that has never been given and will never have the opportunity to be given again, a gift that could indeed propel mankind to the next level of greatness. Effectively it is your ticket to immortality, why wouldn't you pursue it?

We all have a choice
to live a lie
or be ourselves
to laugh and cry
or to follow someone else

to look up and smile
or bow down and frown
to walk the whole mile
or take off our crown

We have a choice
to shout out loud
or chant a whisper
to fly through the clouds
or to be blown like paper

to conquer our fear
or hide in the shadow
to the wise words hear
or be thrown out the window

We all have a choice
to climb our highest mountain
or fall into our deepest hole
to drink from life's fountain
or live life like a troubled soul

to learn love in the heart
or grasp to hate with regret
to wake up and start
or sleep until sunset

We all have a choice
to speak the truth with ourselves
or go against what seems

We all have a choice
to fulfil our greatest dreams

There is someone who wants it more than you do

What do you want and how badly do you want it? Do you dedicate 1 hour a week at it, 1 hour every few days, 1 hour every day, 3 hours every day, 8 hours every day or perhaps 12+ hours every day? The fact is we all want something, but most of us put very little into achieving it. Think of a great musician like Beethoven who was often forced into his room by his drunken father in the early hours of the morning, so he could practice the Piano and Violin all day, or Albert Einstein who sat down for countless hours each day to work on his Theory of relativity. Michael Jordan was the first man on the court and last man to leave for practice every session. For these men and countless other men and women of fame there is no secret formula when it comes to being the best, they just wanted it more than everyone else and got it because they worked at their goals day in, and day out come what may and refused to quit until it was a reality. You might practice being the next Beethoven for 5 hours a day, but the fact is, there is someone out there who is likely practicing 10 hours a day for the same goal, and there is in most cases always going to be someone working harder than you for what they want and the reason they are is because they take full responsibility for their success, they don't make up excuses and give reasons as to why they can't do it, guess what, they damn well find a way to do it. If you say you want something badly enough, there IS going to be competition for it in almost all cases, so you must want it more than anyone else which means you need to find a way to work at it more than anyone else.

If it is important to you, you will find a way. If not, you'll find an excuse.
Ryan Blair

Declutter to stay motivated

Do you spend a vast majority of your time sweating it out around the house trying to get everything done? Do you feel like you waste too much energy on things that don't really matter? Given the opportunity would you simplify your life, so you can have more time to do the awesome activities you actually want to do?

Simplicity is key when staying motivated, and the less material possessions you have, the better. Think about this, if you have a 4-bedroom, 2-bathroom house and there is only 2 or 1 person living in it, think of how much cleaning, dusting, sweeping, moping, and organizing you have to do just to maintain that home. I know because there is a lot of things in my home that have been sitting around for years gathering dust that are not even in use anymore. Basically, they are forgotten assets that act like anchors weighing you down. Why is this important in staying motivated? Remember motivation is like willpower in that it is a finite resource and if you waste it having to look after mundane material possessions then you will use it up more quickly and generally won't have time for your important goals and pursuits. Less is more in this context and you will find firsthand that the more you simplify your life, the more energy and motivation you will have as you will have less to worry about in general and most of what you possess only serves as a distraction from your true purpose. Start by going through your house, even just 1 room at a time and honestly evaluate whether you need that 5 years old broken printer that you stashed away all those years ago or just putting items that have not been used in the last 6 months to one side and later selling them on eBay. You will be amazed at not only how much simpler your life gets and your energy increases but will also likely make some cash on the side. By decluttering your space, you will also declutter your mind and free it up for other creative purposes too. Remember how important it is to simplify your life in every way possible, as this is a key point in staying motivated to achieve your more important goals.

Hard work alone is not enough

A hamster can run up to 9km a night on its wheel according to some experts, damn that's impressive! Hamsters are a great metaphor for this chapter as they explain this point very well. If a goal is described as starting at some point, we will call 'A' and finishing at some point we will call 'B' then a hamster does not really get anywhere! Although yes it does cover a great distance by the end of the night it has gone from point A to point A. Hard work alone is not enough when going after your goals, otherwise most people in society would be exactly where they 'want' to be and not where they currently are. So many of us work tirelessly at our jobs for around 8 hours per days most days of the week, yet how far have we truly gotten? This is basically what the rat race is, it's running on your little hamster wheel known as a "normal life" until we are physically and mentally drained and we are in fact, getting nowhere fast.

I am not suggesting that work is bad or that you should refuse to earn a living, I am just suggesting you really think about where your line of work is taking you. Is it in line with your goals? Does it leave you fulfilled and with more energy when you finish for the day? If the answer is no, then this advice is for you. Hard work is important in anything but what is just as important or even more so is having an action plan for getting there, that way you are not working at nothing.

A good way to illustrate this is to think about going on a road trip, for example from Melbourne to Brisbane, you know that's where you want to go so you consult a map or GPS app on your phone to map out the most efficient route to get there, or you can just get in your car and start driving as quickly as possible in any direction until you drive into the ocean. The second way sounds extreme and absurd, but the reality is most of us live like this. We don't know what we want so we just take something and work extremely hard at it hoping that the map will magically appear to them or they will somehow by pure chance arrive at their destination or close enough to it, unfortunately however, that's not generally how success works in any situation. Therefore, it is vital to sit down and plan your journey before you embark, sit down with your spouse or friends or career advisor and explore different avenues to explore, just like you might Google pictures of certain places you would like to visit before planning to go there.

Remember; plan the steps for your goals first so that your precious hard work will not go to waste.

Your perspiration alone is not enough to make you succeed; you must persevere until every day you break a sweat toward achieving your goals!

Push to the finish line

One of the saddest things about a vast majority of people in the race toward their goals is that they give up just before the finish line.

It is very easy to underestimate just how much effort and resources it takes to accomplish a given task. We all have done it at one time or another. The fact is you will never really know at what point exactly you will reach a goal until you've actually done it. In a 5km marathon you may just start to get tired at the 4km mark and then feel you can't go on after the 4.9km mark, not realizing you only have 100m to go, this is the sad reality of success, it generally occurs just after the cusp of you giving up. It is the final test to see if you really want it bad enough, and most people realize at this stage that they didn't. There is a lot of truth in the saying "Starting is the hardest part" and there is equal truth in saying "Pushing to the finish once you've reached breaking point is just as hard" This is not to discourage you though, this is to encourage you to always just push a little beyond what you believe you can, this is the prelude to personal growth and the prerequisite to success.

It's better to overestimate than underestimate

It's far better to overestimate when it comes to achieving anything worthwhile. This is also paramount to staying motivated. Your direct energy is going to come from the level of preparedness you have allocated to yourself in anything you do, so if you under prepare you are giving yourself a disadvantage to start with. If you are unaware of the amount of time and energy you need to invest in something, don't just blindly assume you know roughly what it takes, look at people who have already achieved something similar to what you are trying to accomplish and learn how they went about it, read a book they may have published and observe their processes, odds are they will have more than adequately prepared for their journey and will give you an advantage over those who don't have the desire to prepare far enough ahead of time. Even if you know how far you need to run so to speak, plan for it as if you were running an even greater distance, why is this important? It's simple, life is full of unexpected setbacks, bumps in the road, and unexpected turns. It's best to overestimate so you are prepared for these events because unfortunately many are not.

Go all in even if you have little to bet

Steve Jobs once said, "We had everything to gain, and we figured even if we crash and burn, and lose everything, the experience will have been worth ten times the cost." How true these words are! Why be afraid to lose $50 when you could potentially make $5000. As a society the fear of losing has been drummed into us from the time we are children, play it safe, don't take big risks, I hear this all too often and it's sickening! I am not suggesting going out and blowing everything on a random bet, what I am saying is don't be afraid to lose what you have to go after what's important to you. You start here with nothing and you leave here with nothing (materially). What matters is the accumulation of fulfilment, contentment, satisfaction, learning experiences and the excitement of the experience. You can always start over no matter what you've lost. Just like a game of poker, what we get to start with is out of our control, we are essentially dealt a hand. Most of us will not even have a pair to start out with whilst a lucky few will be dealt a full house or a straight flush. In the end it doesn't matter what hand you were dealt with, it only matters what you choose to do with it, you can change the hand after the flop as it were and go after the ace and queen you may need for that full house, but whether you get it or not, the joy is in the game itself and how you play it or bluff it. Your life is in your hand and you can always play your hand and win if you know the game well enough, only you can decide whether you have the guts to go all in and achieve what you really want, or fold in fear when it gets too challenging.

A great example of starting off with less-than-ideal cards is Oprah Winfrey, who grew up in poverty and is now a billionaire. She didn't even start with a pair but has grown into a royal flush as it were simply by playing the cards she started with to her advantage and not let anyone stare her down into folding, she created her winning hand by building inner strength and perseverance. Not only her but many other millionaires and billionaires started off with humble means but rather than get discouraged by what they started with, they kept growing and moving forward, challenging their fears, and breaking the barriers that society put before them. Look to them with inspiration as you too move forward and never settle with an average hand, always create your own hand and never be afraid to bet with it.

Weekly Challenge: This week's challenge is all about pushing yourself beyond the boundaries you have given yourself over the years. In this context it could mean you feel you can only jog a certain distance each time you go for a run or giving in to your automatic routines at work or at home. In this challenge you will think of an area of your life that you really want to improve in, something that you have likely been holding off or procrastinating at making steps towards. There is no need to write down any steps you plan on taking, rather you are going to just push yourself to do more and stretch boundaries, such as when you think you have ran out of will power to stop an important task, instead you will just ignore that feelings prodding's and continue anyway, you will likely not like this

at all but that is exactly the point, to break that built up cycle within yourself and to understand that just because your mind says it's had enough, doesn't mean your limits have.

This exercise is aimed at building your willpower and increasing your perceived boundaries to make you realize you are more than the result of what you think you can achieve, world-class athletes constantly break records by this same method, by doing just a little bit more than they did yesterday, and by ignoring the negative voices that whisper in their ear telling them they should stop, they push themselves to greater heights. This is your chance now to push yourself beyond what you were yesterday and beyond what you think you can do now. If you feel uncomfortable with this, then great, it means your stretching your comfort zone and growing your motivation. Start by just doing 10% more than your usual effort, so if you usually run 3km, run 3.3km today, if you spend 5 hours a week on your important project, go for 5.5 this week. You can increase this by 10% each week or each month until you reach a desired level of performance, self-improvement is one of the fundamental steps in motivation and pushing beyond your boundaries is a great first step.

Chapter 5

The race beyond the finish line

Beyond the finish line
there is always
another race,
so never stop running.

You have likely heard the expression "one hit wonder", someone who has become famous for the one and only song they have ever recorded. Think "Kung Fu Fighting" by Carl Douglas or "Macarena" by Los Del Rio. These artists did indeed reach a great finish line in their productions and after that we didn't really hear from them anymore, they reached the end and then…stopped. Even if you do achieve a specific goal there is always other ones to work towards. If you've finally finished your course, then sign up for another one. If you finished reading that book on learning how to sketch, read the next volume and improve those skills, our minds only stop expanding when we stop filling them with the banquet of knowledge, it's only once we stop learning and stop pushing to the next feat that we stop our overall progress. The number of marathons in your life is determined by you and you alone, so don't limit yourself to the standard one marathon that most people take, the marathon of getting a 'standard job' and a 'standard mortgage' and associate with 'standard people' who do 'standard things' just to fit in. Create your own standard of success in your unique marathon(s), and just because you finish one, don't limit yourself, plan the next one and never stop running even beyond the finish line.

The more you do the more energy you will have

It may see to counter-intuitive but it's true, the more you do, the more energy you will have. You can test this by sitting on the couch watching TV all day and discover by the time you've been vegging for 3 hours you basically can't even get up! You feel like just drifting off to sleep. This works almost the same as overexerting yourself, where you just want to collapse on the nearest surface and sleep for the next 12 hours. When I first started jogging most days, I would jog in one session of 30 to 45 minutes in the morning just after getting out of bed. I found this ok at the start but after I had finished, I would get tired after a couple of hours. I found though that if I split my exercise over 3 shorter sessions of between 10 and 15 minutes throughout the day, I had a more constant source of energy, and conversely the more exercise I did, the more energized I felt. But don't stop there, once you've completed one task for the day go straight to the next after rewarding yourself with something you enjoy or having a small break to be in nature. If you don't have anything else planned, then plan something to do next, something meaningful and important to you. You will find very rapidly that applying this on a daily basis will start to give you rivers of energy and motivation. The more you do, the more successful you will feel and as a result the more motivated you will feel to keep going.

Change up your marathon

Just because you have consistently run one type of marathon does not mean you are locked into that marathon for the rest of your life. Peter Garrett, lead singer of the famous Aussie Rock band Midnight Oil changed his marathon to politics after his band's music success. Now he is the minister of education and effecting positive change for the education system of students throughout Australia and has done so for many years now. If you are bored with your current race, swap to a new one, take the next exit and start something new that you have always wanted to. If you are in retail and have always wanted to be pursuing the Guitar, then what's stopping you? Don't make up excuses and say it's too late, after all some people don't find their passions until they're 50 or older, some don't find it at all. Don't be like those people, start pursuing your awesomeness now! Don't wait, do it now, stop reading and start doing it and you will never regret it.

Don't run someone else's marathon

The majority of mankind is and has been the minorities' marathon for thousands of years, way back in the times of Ancient Egypt up until now. Who are these runners? Most are not well known. For years I ran many different marathons that were not my own, and guess what? Not once did I ever win one! If you run someone else' marathon whether it be you trying to be like them, work for their company, or just trying to impress them for whatever reason, then STOP! The only marathon you can ever hope to win is your own, the only race you will win gold, is your own, the only marathon you can complete is none but your own. So, stop trying to live someone else's dream and chase their visions, because you will never be fulfilled. I have never been happier following my own path and running my own race, because at least then, I can tell the story and I can sweat my own success, not someone else's.

By no means am I saying just pack in your job, family or anything that is important to you, but it is never too late to plan your marathon and start taking steps to achieve that, no matter what it takes. You don't need some special start in life to be your own leader, you need to be courageous enough to make the first step, accept that failure is temporary and beneficial for you, and the unwavering belief in yourself that you can achieve it and will achieve it sooner or later. Don't be afraid to take risks, most people are too afraid to take risks and as a result, end up running a safe race with someone else's end goal in mind. The biggest risk is not investing in yourself and your uniqueness, embrace it and run your marathon the way you want to.

> *Your time is limited, so don't waste*
> *it living someone else's life.*
> Steve Jobs

Obsession is not necessarily a bad thing

When Passion meets
Inspiration
An obsession
Is born
RVM

What comes to your mind when you think of the word 'obsession'? Maybe it holds a negative connotation to you, or perhaps you think of someone who is determined to achieve something and will stop at nothing to get it. The dictionary defines it as "an idea or thought that continually preoccupies or intrudes on a person's mind." Ask any person in life who has truly achieved success in their goals, and they will probably tell you that it was always on their mind. They'll always say they preoccupied their minds with that goal, they may allude to the word 'obsession' but what they are telling you is that to them, their goal, dream or vision was an obsession. If you are the best at something, and that's all you do with your free time, it becomes your obsession, and that's not a bad thing. Michael Jordan, Tiger Woods, Bill Gates, Arnold Schwarzenegger, Oprah Winfrey, Steve Jobs, Warren Buffet and many other successful people in any field, the one quality that separated them from the rest was their degree of obsession to their goals. Much like I mentioned before, if you think about the routines of these inspirational magnates, you will see a common theme; Michael Jordan was the first in the gym each day and the last person to leave – great obsession. Steve Jobs worked at his dream for 15 hours a day 7 days a week, you can be sure that those who get to the top, get there on purpose, not by mere chance, it isn't just that they outworked their competition, it's the fact that their vision never escaped their minds, not even for a moment. They thought about their goals and their processes before they went to bed each night. First thing upon waking up the next morning, each day, each week, year-round, to the point where that process became second nature and habitual to them, their vision was already a reality to them, it was just a matter of time to see the results.

How do you know you have this degree of obsession? It will start to exude from you and spill on to everyone you come into contact with, and you will not even realize this because you will be too busy living the journey of that goal and seeing its realization as the juiciest fruit produced by the plant you worked so hard to cultivate. Remember that when it comes to achieving your goal and staying motivated that obsession is one of your greatest allies and will become apparent not only by the fruits of your labour but also by the fact that it will energize and inspire those around you too.

Lessons from Forest Gump

If you have ever seen the movie Forest Gump, you will know just how inspirational the film is. There is so much we can learn from this brilliant man in how he lived his life and how he stayed motivated.

Firstly, he did not over think things, and for this many in the film would call him "slow" or "stupid", when really this was not the case at all, if Forest wanted something like to run for 3 years and 2 months across the whole of America, he just did it. When he finished his college degree and was invited to join the army, he did it. The lesson here is though it is wise to think large decisions through before making them, it won't do you any good to over think yourself into a mental paralysis and end up making zero decisions, this is how you miss opportunities in life and we all likely have at some point because of thinking too much about it, I know I certainly have.

Secondly Forest was a man of his word. When he said he would become a first mate on a shrimping boat to his friend who later died in the film, he remembered that promise and became a captain instead. When he found out that he had a son he said he would look after him and he did. Most of us are guilty of making promises we have not kept for one reason or another, the point is if you want to stay motivated and taken seriously by those who care about you then you best keep your word when you give it. Keeping your word builds a strong sense of character, especially in a world where the average new year's resolution barely lasts a month before it is abandoned. The more often you keep your word too, the more self-respect you feel toward yourself, the more you will take yourself seriously, and the stronger you will become in becoming a person of habit.

Thirdly Forest followed his heart. He did not cave in to the demands of a 'you should' society. He became a pro football star, a pro ping pong champion, investor in Apple, owned a successful shrimping business, became a war hero and met three presidents. True, this is not based on actual events but that does not mean there is no take away from this story. From birth on we start being programmed by the coding's of society, we are taught rules and laws and how to fit into the crowd, we are taught to just get a job and buy a house, save for retirement, and play it safe. Think how much more diverse and happy society would be if instead we were taught values and compassion, how to embrace our uniqueness and create opportunities rather than just join someone else's. The fact is though we can and it's never too late to start learning who you are and what you value in life. That search is yours and yours alone but realize that it's never too late to start, and the sooner you start your own path, the more motivated you will feel.

Run beyond the finish line

Perhaps you have completed your project or are at least very close, in any case never settle for a one marathon race, you likely put in arduous amounts of time, preparation and work into your first goal, and you want to keep that momentum rolling so it's easier to start the next one. Just like a real marathon takes time, planning and effort, you will be prepared for that particular race, but if you finish it and then stop all together, your stamina and determination start to dwindle into inactivity and the mind becomes stagnant. Although yes it is still possible to start over, it takes a lot more effort, time and willpower to get to that par level you were initially on, that's why it's so important to keep running even after the finish line and keep that same momentum into the next race, because likely your next goal will challenge you even more than your first goal did, so getting that head start will only serve as an advantage to you. In the end whatever results come your way it is far better to meet a failure in the middle of a race than to meet defeat in the presence of inaction. Better to meet setbacks on your home stretch than finding resignation just before commencement, in other words it's better to always be achieving something, no matter how trivial towards a much grander goal. Better to make it even an inch closer to the finishing ribbon. Best to be afraid whilst running than petrified by the prospect of starting and failing. People may discourage you, not believe in you or oppose you, even if they do take it in good measure, for then at least you know you are doing something that others dare not for the same scourge of disbelief. The marathon they quit or refused to start is testament to the fact that they despise your efforts and your blatant refusal to settle for a life of mediocrity.

Settle for nothing less than the wealth and prosperity you deserve!

Learn from the trials of your marathon

We also exult
In our tribulations,
Knowing that tribulation
Brings about perseverance;
Romans 5:3

You are running along on your merry marathon; the fresh morning breeze caresses your hair with the touch of freedom; the path in which you tread applauds your feet with every step as you inhale the ocean's familiar scent. Then suddenly you trip on a rock and sprain your ankle, you fall to the floor in a moment of defeat and perhaps some outbursts of profanity. A cloud of disappointment settles upon your head as you think that it's probably best to call it a day. This example is not the exception to the rule of any challenge in life, it is the rule. You will face setbacks and sprains of many sorts on basically all of your ventures, but rather than view that as the thorn bush that holds you back when you brush past it, you would fair far better by learning from it and viewing it for what it really is… your motivation tester. If you face a small setback and quit, then it's probably a good indication that you probably didn't really want it that much in the first place. If you love your marathon enough, nothing will hold you back from finishing it, if you trip and get a sprain you will get back up and finish even if you have to limp to the finish line holding your tongue.

Successful people refuse to make excuses to stop them from their end goal. They don't let small or large setbacks hinder them, instead they use them to build perseverance and grow into a stronger obstacle annihilator that has the finish line constantly at the forefront of their minds and hearts and never quit. Remember to keep your eyes in front of you and prepare for potential obstacles and setbacks, see them before a fall if you can and take action but even if you should trip, keep in mind that obstacles are actually beneficial for your goals, as they test the level of heart you have invested in them.

Tribulations build perseverance, perseverance builds progress, and progress eventually builds greatness and success.

Weekly Challenge: This week's challenge is a self-check exercise to see whether you are finishing a goal and actively planning the next goal. By this point you should be comfortable with the concept of smaller goals creating larger goals over time. You will need to ask yourself some questions, first being, have I been consistent in achieving my smaller goals over the last few weeks? What sort of challenges have I been facing and how have I reacted to them? Am I being realistic in my expectations? It is very common to experience many setbacks and resistance when you start planning even small goals, especially if you are not used to doing it.

If you found that you are completing goals easily with time to spare, then by all means increase the scope of your goals and make it a goal to spend more time on them, if you find you are struggling with your goals for whatever reason, don't beat yourself up, even if you've been procrastinating, make your goals smaller and smaller until you do achieve one, this is because you want to get accustomed with that dopamine sense of accomplishment, no matter how tiny it is. When you complete a goal, it motivates you to do it again, and you will start to naturally move towards larger goals. Here are the steps to take this week.

1. Self-evaluate from your last few weeks and check your progress
2. Identify areas that are strong or that need improvement

3. Increase the amount of time you spend on your goals if you are finding them currently too easy and not fulfilling enough
4. If you are procrastinating or just generally overloaded, don't beat yourself up, instead reduce the size of your goals until you can achieve them realistically
5. Once you do achieve your goal, gradually increase the scope of that goal to challenge yourself and push your boundaries.

Chapter 6

Rebuilding yourself from your design

Never be afraid
To fall apart
Because it is an
Opportunity to rebuild yourself
The way you wish
You had been all
Along.
Rae Smith

The world we occupy is one in which is constantly building itself and then tearing itself down from season to season, year to year, century to century, millennia to millennia. Nature is the perfect recycling system and wastes nothing in its process. Nature expunges the waste and the useless materials that no longer serve to become symbiotic with its ecosystem. Maggots exists to aid in the disposal of the dead carcasses, flies help to break down the biological waste of other creatures, and because sharks exist on the top of the food chain, they aid in keeping the oceans well balanced by controlling the populations of other marine species. Every part of nature serves a purpose in the overall survival of our entire ecosystem and this process of breaking down and rebuilding is at the forefront of that. As soon as one species becomes extinct, our ecosystem as a whole suffers as now a unique role that was filled by that species is no longer catered for, this can in effect bounce on to other species that may be dependent to some extent on the services of that extinct species. The point is clear, the delicate balance of nature is there by design and its systems apply equally to humans as a species too.

Likely you have someone you know who always seems to win and succeed at whatever they do, you might think how great it must be, but is it really? Winning is great but generally we learn very little from it, such as areas we can improve in. Usually too people who are used to winning are usually hit the hardest when they finally lose at something, it can damage their moral in such a way that recovery is more difficult than for most. Let's go in the other direction, say your used to falling short at just about everything you seem to do, you may feel like a failure or have the attitude of 'why bother', I have been there many times, and yes, it is not a nice way to feel by any means. One thing you learn though is that the more you fail, the more creative you seem to get. You start to see things most if not all other people miss, you gain a sense of awareness that becomes unparalleled and unique thinking patterns start to take over.

Say you purchase a 120-year-old house and want to rebuild it; do you just start working over the existing house and start laying tiles on the roof that is now mostly corroded and covered in rust? Sure, you could just build on top of the previous foundation but will the household up over time? more than likely not. A new house built on an old, outdated foundation is sure to fail the moment you slam the front door too hard. Much in the same way if your lifestyle is full of unhelpful habits and built on painful past experiences and you try to build on that foundation, you are only setting yourself up for the eventual collapse of your wellbeing.

I am not suggesting letting yourself completely fall apart but to accept that falling apart can be a great opportunity to redefine yourself in the way you actually want, not the way society may have moulded you over the years. View it as nature's way of tearing down the 'old' you in order to make way for the 'new' improved you. Even what you consider to be a minor setback might be an opportunity for you to create a major breakthrough, and if you are having what you perceive as a major breakdown, it may just be the ticket for you to change your life into something you would never have imagined in your previous mindset. Oprah Winfrey, Mark Cuban and Steve Jobs were all fired from their positions before they rose to wealth, and for them it was the breakdown they needed to achieve their respective breakthroughs. Sure, it is disheartening to receive the 50th rejection email in a row from jobs you have applied for or to have someone you care about leave you, but this is not the end, rather the start of your own new beginning to be who you want to be and motivate yourself on your own terms and conditions.

Remember, Failure is not great, but sometimes it is necessary. We all learn many habits over a lifetime and sadly most are not helpful ones; smoking, excessive drinking, all sorts of addictions, you name it. The only reason we have learnt to avidly dislike failure is because we have grown up in society that places a dogma of worthlessness on it, when really failure can, and is often necessary for success and growth to a new and better you, as well as motivating you to strive for better and learn creating ways of challenging existing issues. Let setbacks and failures in your life be the decomposition of old out-dated habits and allow the blossom of new improved habits to take over from them. Embrace your failures and never stop moving forward to success!

Learn a lesson from the hare and the tortoise

You are likely familiar with the tale of the hare and the tortoise.

The hare and tortoise have a race in which the hare has a clear unfair advantage, the hare races off so far ahead and decides to take a nap in a moment of complacency. To the hare's amazement when he finally wakes up the tortoise has crossed the finish line and wins the race. This is a great lesson on pacing yourself and being mindful of complacency. If you are starting an exciting goal in which you are passionate about, it is tempting just to race off ahead and finish it as quickly as possible. However, be mindful of this approach as what occurs all too often is fatigue. Putting an abundance of energy into a fulfilling task is great, however putting in too much energy too quickly could potentially lead to burnout and complacency later, in which the hare known as your rival, your motivational block, will eventually overtake you. Remember this lesson always as by pacing yourself realistically on your race; you stand a far better chance to maintain your energy and passion towards your goal, rather than going for the all-out sprint only to realize the journey will likely take longer than you anticipated.

Examples of motivational suicide

Rate yourself honestly in the following areas, 10 being 'I never do that' and 1 being 'I do that all the time'

- Comparing yourself to others
- Doing too many things at once
- Trying to please everyone
- Not looking after yourself
- Constantly looking to the past or future
- General usage of the words 'should' or 'shouldn't.'
- Holding on to grudges and resentments
- Not challenging yourself
- Remaining stagnant
- Harbouring the useless emotion of 'regret.'
- Having no goals
- Not planning steps to achieve your goals
- Not visualizing my goals frequently enough

Healthy behaviours that boost motivation

Prioritize these honestly starting in areas you feel it would be most appropriate to work on first with 1 being 'I need to start this

ASAP' to 5 being 'I can benefit from working on this area, but it is not urgent' put NA if not applicable.

- Comparing myself only to myself from a previous time
- Doing one thing at a time and doing it to the best of my ability
- Be myself, be reasonable, and not try to please everyone
- Take better care of my health both physically and emotionally
- Being more mindful of the present moment and living in the now
- Changing disempowering words like 'should' and 'shouldn't' to words like 'It might not be wise to…' or 'I can if I do this…'
- Letting go of grudges and resentment as I realize they are only harming me in the end
- Challenge me to always improve myself and be the best version of myself
- Getting more active both mentally and physically as I realize that being healthy in body and mind is the cornerstone of staying motivated.
- Quickly recognizing the emotion of regret and realizing it really is a useless emotion that only saps motivation and causes me to dwell on the past which I cannot change
- Create some positive and realistic goals for myself as this will give me something to focus my creative energy on and improve myself constantly
- Once I have a concrete and realistic goal in mind actively planning how I am going to go about turning that into a reality
- Keeping physical images or my goal and its successful completion on hand at all times and actively visualizing it's completion before I go to bed each night and first thing when I wake up in the morning

Rebuild yourself with kindness

  We all likely want to better ourselves in some way. Often, it is common to say things to yourself like 'I should be better at this by now' or 'I shouldn't still have this – 'Insert undesired trait'- in my life. The more we talk to our self like this, the more unrealistic expectation we create for our self. This brings more pressure we put onto what we think we should be. Thus, the unhappier we start to feel. Remember that these words and self-talk are largely what is destroying us in the first place. This is exactly the kind of language we should aspire to move away from. Just as you want to rebuild a house with strong, quality bricks, you want to treat yourself the same way, by rebuilding with compassion for what you have already achieved and what you can still achieve.

  Having realistic and small goals to start with will ensure that you are making constant progress toward who you strive to be. If at any point while you are working on yourself you notice that you are becoming unhappy, look at what you are saying to yourself and what expectations you have towards yourself. Likely you are placing too much burden on your level of progress; you may also find yourself using the words 'should' and 'shouldn't' more often in which you want to catch yourself in this act ASAP. Expecting too much too quickly is a speedy way to start tearing down the progress you have already made in rebuilding you in your image, so be kind and patient with yourself and let this happen naturally. There is not a set time you need to complete yourself in as in essence it is a lifelong journey anyway.

Rebuilt with self-awareness

I think self-awareness
is probably the most important thing
towards being a champion
-Billie Jean King

Being kind to yourself is a great way to start rebuilding yourself and what is equally important is self-awareness. The ability to know yourself, your strengths, weaknesses, values, and passion, knowing when you have made a mistake and how to fix it, these all form the core of your self-awareness. If you are not quite sure on some of these things, then it's important that you take the time to think about them and meditate on them, for how are you supposed to rebuild if you don't know what to rebuild with. Self-awareness is the equivalent to knowing the type of brick, size of brick, shape of brick, colour of brick and brand of brick that you want to build your new house with. Naturally, there is a lot of options here but it's a case of observation of your minds focal point, you will know it when you see it, and you will see it if you observe your thoughts and feelings over time, the heart reveals itself in subtle and prodding ways, so those of us who have learned to drown out our intuitions through mindless tasks and distractions become far less sensitive to its persistent calling. This is why I say you must allow yourself the time to sit with yourself and observe without judgment where your inclinations and thoughts take you; they provide vital clues to figuring out your desires and become audible when we become quiet within ourselves. Self-awareness is not so much a skill to be learned though it is something we would be wise to allow time to practice the art of internal silence to hear the voice that exists beyond the clutter of thoughts that litter our mind in a typical day.

Perhaps the biggest obstacle that hinders self-awareness is comparing yourself to someone else and their values and lifestyle, this is because one's own personal experiences primarily influence their own values, and everyone's personal experiences are greatly varied. Self-awareness is a type of discipline and disciple is not acquired by stark imitation of another person's discipline, whether it's noble or not. Discipline implies not only trained skill but a trained attitude and appreciation for the context of one's acquired skills. It's that degree of self-awareness that enables the appreciation of those attitudes and the acquisition of those unique values. Therefore, you want to develop your values through your own practiced discipline and life experiences.

Rebuild yourself with the cement of practice

What's the best way to master a skill? Practice. Practice is to progress as cement is to brick. So, you know what you want, what your strengths and weakness are, what you value, now it's time to start practising, over and over again until the new desired 'you' becomes the automatic 'you' that doesn't have to guess themselves at every second corner. It may sound obvious that it takes practice in order to improve, which is not 'million dollar' advice so to speak. The order in which you practice something is important, that is why I mention it after being kind to yourself and having a high degree of self-awareness, because practising the wrong skills and values to you is detrimental to your overall motivation, whereas practising the skills and traits you actually want and the specific values you wish to improve on is vital.

Just as practising the incorrect technique of an aerobic move can cause injury to your body, the incorrect motivation for achieving any goal will only lead you down the wrong path. What I specifically mean here is why you are doing what you are doing. If you want to improve the overall quality of your life then this is a fantastic motivator, if you are doing it to impress random people you associate with, just know that superficial reasons for anything are short-lived and not in line with your true values, therefore subconsciously you will keep finding ways to sabotage yourself. Practice only the values you truly want for yourself and know why you want what you choose to pursue.

Rebuild yourself with the right connections

Surround
Yourself with

> *Only people*
> *Who are*
> *Going to lift*
> *You higher.*
> *-Oprah Winfrey*

We as humans are social beings; we derive a great portion of our life experiences both with and through other people, as such it is one of the most influential aspects in our development both emotionally and cognitively. Good associations can be the difference between staying motivated to achieve your goals and staying motivated to waste time and procrastinate. Choose your friends wisely, especially if you constantly find yourself in a crisis around certain people, it is no accident that you find yourself getting nowhere around certain people, and if this is you then get out as soon as possible.

You may think that you can have a positive influence on their self-destructive behaviours, but in most cases, they are going to end up slowly changing you into the direction of a void-filled life deplete of any real meaning. Studies have shown that you will end up earning roughly the average of your 5 closest friends (again no accident). It therefore stands to reason that your associations are not only going to rub off on your levels of motivation, but they are also going to average out among the people you choose to have in your life. This will be true if you have mixed positive and negative friends. If you blend with them all equally enough you will average out like the alkalinity of water that has half acids and half bases in the mix.

Just like Oprah said, you want to surround yourself with people who lift you, not tear you down and it's quite easy to identify, ask yourself if you feel more energized and more of an elevated mood after you have spent time with a certain friend/s. What do you immediately feel like doing once you've finished spending time together; If you feel drained and tired either mentally or physically you want to notice what about your contact with them has left you feeling this way. If you feel inspired and energised to better yourself and are more motivated to keep pursuing positive outcomes then likely this person/s has not only similar values to you but also has your sense of discipline, drive, and consistency that is conducive to progress.

Addictions and staying motivated

Addictions interact in a unique way with motivation. Addictions are in effect a form of destructive motivation that produces a physical response in the body. Every time you indulge yourself and give in to addictive behaviour your brain releases dopamine, a powerful feel-good chemical that acts as the reward to the addiction, this is what makes breaking addictions often quite challenging. Resisting the brain's cry to satisfy an addiction is akin to wrestling a hungry lion. You might be able to hold off for a while but sooner or later, you will run out of strength. Trying to control an addiction will therefore drain you of motivation very quickly and even when you give in to its vices, your brain will signify through the dopamine response that now it has what it longed for and there is no need to remain in a state of high motivation. Having said that, if addictions are a form of motivation, then they can be overcome using motivation detours, i.e., rerouting the addiction to a more productive habit that will benefit your specific goal. This still will take time and effort but the more you redirect your addictive behaviour to habit building, the easier it will become. Don't let addictions run your life and it's always wise to seek professional help in addition to this to make the process smoother and quicker for yourself to overcome.

Planning too far ahead

If you focus too intently
On the path you have planned

> You might not see the angry bear
> Hunting just outside her lair

Say you have just approached the beginning of a large forest with a long pathway that leads to the other side. You want to get through the forest as quickly as possible with little distraction, you fix your eager eyes firmly on the last tree before the forest ends and never take your eyes off that focal point. You get to the halfway mark of the forest with your eyes still glued to that same tree in anticipation, so much so that you don't see the angry grizzly whose lair you have just carelessly stumbled by. You still have your eyes fixed to the tree before you are knocked down and assaulted by the defensive bear.

You notice just before you hit the ground that there are signs everywhere warning of bears in the area, but you were too focused on the endpoint to notice them. The lesson here is not to be too focused and fixed on one point in your journey that is almost too far off to see when you should have your attention fixed on the signs and obstacles that present a threat earlier on, obstacles such as self-doubt, fear, procrastination and so many more. It is wise to look at your end goal from time to time, but only enough so it keeps you fuelled and motivated. Your main focus is the steps in front of you and how you walk them.

Now, we have already discussed the importance of planning when it comes to motivation, but you still want to be careful not to plan too far ahead. Think of a new year's resolution again and almost entirely how unsuccessful they generally are, and it's no wonder! We likely have this huge goal that we want to achieve by the end of the year. The problem with this mindset is that it lacks a sense of urgency to complete. If, for instance, you have a year to complete a task you may be able to achieve in a matter of a few months, you are subconsciously telling your brain that you have more than enough time to complete this goal. I can, therefore, take it slow for a few weeks or months. Another problem with this is life's inherent notoriety for unpredictability. If something important enough happens in those weeks or months (and it usually does), your brain pushes older goals into the back burner and are at this stage, mostly forgotten and become the ill-fated regret of next year's resolution. Deadlines that you give yourself that are reasonable and not too far away will subconsciously prime your brain with a hard sense of urgency, especially if you have it in writing. A sensible break down approach would be to apply these steps for planning and executing goals.

- Create hourly plans that count toward a daily plan
- Incorporate these daily plans in weekly plans
- Use these weekly plans to move you closer to monthly plans
- Monthly plans to longer-term plans

A daily plan is realistic and achievable, but you have to use your hourly plans productively and well scheduled out, remembering to include rest breaks hourly. Long term plans only lose their validity once the shorter-term plans start breaking away and are not realistic or appropriate for a specific goal. This is why short-term goals are so important toward long term goals, as they will help you to identify any issue quickly rather than later on down the road. Having a calendar to check your progress weekly will make this an even more simple process to navigate. Remember short term planning is important to staying motivated, short terms goals should coincide with longer-term goals and act as checkpoints along the way to their eventual fulfilment. Be mindful of not planning too far ahead as this can bring about complacency and destroy the motivation that a keen sense of urgency provides. Also planning too far ahead can cause tunnel vision in our acquisition of our goal and therefore miss potential opportunities to improve our process along the way.

Open-mindedness

Aim for the experience
of a professional,
With the curiosity
Of a beginner

To specialise in any skill is a celebration-worthy experience. Generally, though it comes at a price…rigid mindedness. To specialize in any field typically takes the better half of a decade. The specialist will be focusing intently on a specific area in a particular field which requires defined skill sets, mindsets, and practices, because it is specialized with a high degree of precision in its realization. The specialist usually develops a strong sense of black and white thinking in which, it is this way and this way only. In effect, her creativity becomes dormant as the thought of another way of doing something becomes absurd. This leads to rigidity in thinking in which logical persuasion cannot penetrate the stiffness of the minds trained thinking, they have learned to think autonomously with their years of training and thus dare not question it. A strong key in open-mindedness is self-awareness and observation without judgment of your environment, It is important to let your overall skill set guide you, but not blind you, in other words, you want to make sure you are in control of your thinking patterns and degree of consciousness in the work you do, if your work satisfies you, it means your consciously aware of your creative ability acting independently of your autonomous self.

Happiness precedes Success, not the other way around

Stop waiting
For Friday,
For Summer,
For someone

> *To fall in love with you,*
> *For life.*
> *Happiness*
> *Is achieved when*
> *You stop waiting for it*
> *And make the most*
> *Of the moment you're in now.*
> *-Unknown*

Have you ever said to someone or yourself? "I will be happy when I have (insert future event) in my life." Most people have at some point more than likely than not because we live in a day and age where people equate 'things' or 'certain outcomes' to happiness, yet so many well-meaning people in the world today seem to be lost when it comes to what does induce this much sought out state of mind. According to one source happiness is a sense of well-being or contentment and is a by-product of success, safety, or luck. Sure, such events can be cause for a lot of joy, but there are also many who are successful in business, relationships and other pursuits that are also unhappy. For the most part, most of Western society lives in relative safety, yet a large majority suffer Depression and general displeasure with life, and luck, well luck rarely lasts that long anyway and a large number of so-called lucky people such as lottery winner's end up worse off than when they acquired their lucky wealth.

These factors can play a considerable role in our level of happiness, yet many possess none of these and still live in a state of constant gratitude and consistent joy with life. So, what separates these individuals from the vast populous? It may be what they do not possess that causes their higher levels of general happiness towards life. Again, the issue appears to stem from 'distractions.' It is almost considered a crime within oneself to be 'not-busy', a state of mind in which we don't feel taxed enough by our current situation and therefore have the urge to purge this unwelcome sensation and do something for show or just for the sake of it. In an on-the-go society, it seems to lack sense to ever be 'not-busy', we go from activity to activity seeking the next injection of stimulation, just like a drug, and overuse of any addictive substance invites trouble. The desire to alleviate this feeling of not being busy enough is in many ways similar to an itch that warrants a scratch. It feels good, but keep scratching, and soon you will harbor a rash. Even more sinister is its similarity to the symptoms one would get from heroin withdrawal. It keeps getting more painful to resist the longer you leave it unsatisfied. Much like the body needs physical rest after an intense workout, so does the mind need rest after intense planning or over-stimulation. The need therefore to always have your mind stimulated and acting on this through mindless distraction is akin to completing a 1-hour intense cardio session and then saying, "well I may as well not stop until I collapse and end up in the ER" otherwise I will have energy left over in my body that will start to irritate me".

Although you will likely not experience the same effects as this example, give yourself enough time to be constantly overstimulated and you will eventually drive yourself into some form of mental illness or mental breakdown. The mind needs to be free from tasks from time to time just like our bodies need to take it easy for a while after intense activity. Allowing time not to be busy has been shown by many studies to increase creativity substantially and help people to come up with unique and innovative solutions to problems that they could not otherwise solve. So how does one allow them the luxury of this freedom then? Well, much like overcoming any addiction, start by allowing more time away from the need to instantly fix 'busyness.'

Slowly detoxify yourself from this impulse and allow yourself a small amount of time each day to 'be' with yourself and enjoy the moment, this is basically what mindfulness meditation is, being in the present moment and engaging your senses to the present environment. See it, smell it, taste it, feel it, and hear it without judgment. You will soon find yourself with the inevitable feeling of stationary tension. Do not judge that feeling either, let it be there and feel what stillness physically feels like. If you do this even for just 5 minutes a day, you will notice that being less busy is actually not a bad thing at all, and the clarity within yourself will be greatly increased in a short time if you keep practising it. Remember your mind needs a break when it is constantly stimulated just as the body needs rest after physical activity. Allow yourself time to be free from activity every day even for just 5 minutes to increase your mental clarity which will, in turn, will help you stay motivated.

Weekly Challenge: This challenge is all about mindfulness and reducing your level of 'busyness' in your life. Start this week with just 5 minutes each day to be still and engage with your senses. Watch the sunset as you smell the fresh afternoon Seabreeze or simply sit outside and feel the rain or wind on your skin and don't place any judgement on it. The purpose of this exercise is to get the full experience of all of your bodily sensations and not judge a single one of them, this will help your mind to quiet down and cleanse your conscious mind, helping it focus on what's in front of you. Do this for 5 minutes each day for the first week and then increase it by a few minutes each week until you are happy with your level of awareness. If you are more in line with your physical sensations, your mind will follow suit and staying motivated becomes much easier because you can visualize your goals to a much higher degree, and you will find your focus on planning and achieving these goals becomes much smoother overall.

Chapter 7

Staying Motivated in a World of Increasing Challenges

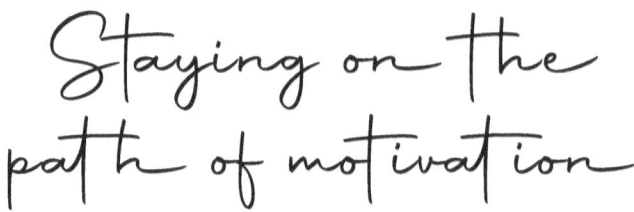
Staying on the path of motivation

> You didn't come
> This far
> To only come
> This far
> -Unknown

Let's start with an analogy. Think of a balloon that your child decides to fill with one small breath of air, he holds the opening for a moment, then lets it fly, it barely moves a foot. Now suppose he blows and blows on it until it is ready to burst, holds it for a moment and then releases, it shoots off 15 feet across the room, hits the roof, the dining table, comes back around, knocks over a desk lamp and then flies off another 25 feet before hitting the floor. Think of your motivation like that balloon that you fill with your every breath. What output you get is directly proportional to the input of energy you put every step of your goal, most give their balloons 1 single breath here and there then release the balloon expecting great results only to find it barely goes the length of a room and yet remain disappointed and blame the balloon for not getting very far. Most try to fill someone else balloon with their precious air and wonder why the breath they have left over for their balloon is insufficient for any real momentum. Fill your balloon first, so you give it the best quantity and quality air to stay motivated. Let's have a look at some of the different ways you fill your balloon first.

- Waking up and displaying gratitude for what you do have

- Feeding your body nutritious food on a regular basis
- Exercising your body to increase your energy
- Not trying to please every person you walk past
- Taking time every day to enjoy your own company
- Making progress toward your bigger goals every day by creating and accomplishing smaller goals that count toward your larger goal
- Staying connected with people who have your best interests at heart and encourage you to persevere through challenges
- Taking pride in yourself and how you present yourself
- Taking pride in the things that matter to you
- Not settling for anything less than you know you are worthy of

Gratitude puts you into a positive state of mind which mentally energizes you for the day ahead.

Feeding your body with nutritious food regularly will give your body the physical energy to face the day, obvious yet often not applied by many.

Exercising your body increases your body's BDNF (Brain-derived neurotrophic factor), which will help your brain create more neurons and neural connections, as well as boost your endorphins which lead to a sense of happiness and increased physical and mental energy.

People pleasing robs us of valuable energy as it requires, we constantly use valuable motivational energy to transform into a different person to cater for other people's tolerances, if someone doesn't like you for you, move on, it's as simple as that.

Taking time to yourself may seem selfish. Depending on how you look at it, but really, it's not, taking time for yourself each day to do what you want to do increases your peace of mind and helps you to de-stress. When you're not stressed, you have increased energy and motivation, and when you're not as stressed you can do more for others, so really, it's actually not selfish at all.

Trying to move toward a large goal without having smaller goals to bring you closer to that goal is like trying to move a trailer load of sand in one shover full. For one it's not going to happen, two, you will hurt yourself, and three, you will give up quickly. Think of your smaller goals as shovelling one manageable scoop of sand at a time and piling it in the area where you want the pile to end up when you're done, i.e., your larger goal.

Associating yourself with like-minded people who actually care about your vision is critically important. These people will be the determining factor when you have nowhere else to turn to after hitting a wall and need encouragement. A good friend will not only help you stay on track but actively help you back on your feet while a mock friend will not give two hoots whether you achieve your goals or not. So be mindful who you allow in your life, they will either be the sturdy bridge that allows you over your river of defeat, or a broken bridge ready to fail just as you step onto it. A great friend will always be a source of energy and support.

How you present yourself is a direct representation of how you subconsciously feel about yourself. If you get up in the morning on the weekend and stay in your P. J's all day, not grooming your hair or brushing your teeth, skipping showers every other day and slouched over with a poor posture, you likely don't care about yourself or your goals that much to try to achieve them. Even if no one is around when you still try to look your best every day and respect yourself, you are going to be far more motivated and driven then someone who neglects this simple step.

If the activities in your life don't bring you joy, find a way to remove them from your life. If you find that you never put your all into something, it's very likely the task you are doing is not meaningful to you and doesn't energize you. For this reason, you need to explore multiple avenues or your values and passions until you find something that genuinely excites you. Simply put, if you are not passionate about something, and it gives you little or no joy, you will probably only give it 30% of your potential effort. If you love what you do, even if it takes you a long time to find it, you will not only put in 100%, you will likely strive to go above and beyond expectation and drive yourself to the status of legends, find what you love and make it your passion.

Never settle for anything, settling represents the mindset of a quitter, and quitters are not motivated people, don't be one of them. We are all worth a 5-star meal so to speak, when we settle, we are in essence ordering that top-quality rump steak and when the waiter comes out and hands you an undercooked party pie, you accept it!

It's absurd, but sadly a vast majority of people do accept that wrong order and ration off what they can with what they were given, aiming for the best and never settling is the way champions motivate themselves consistently.

Kaizen

The word Kaizen is a Japanese word that effectively means constant and never-ending improvement. It was adopted after the second world war and applied mainly to business but encompasses many aspects of people lives throughout the world. The idea behind it, specifically in industry and logistics, was to involve all members of the product line, from CEO to general workers, in the process of improving themselves and as a result, improving productivity and moral throughout the workforce, thus minimizing waste. By constantly striving to improve your own life through gaining new skills, practicing new ways of doing things, meditation, exercise, diet, and many other avenues you will find by adopting the idea of constantly improving yourself not only gives you more motivation but helps you to weed out more of the wasteful activities that clutter your time.

How you live is your choice

You always have a choice, and right now the only thing holding you back from achieving anything you feel you lack in is you and you alone. The overall message in this book is that challenging yourself daily will be the greatest source of your motivation and your motivation will continue to grow if you continue to challenge yourself to be a better version of yourself than yesterday. Sometimes the hardest thing to do as humans is to accept responsibility for where we are at present. Many things are out of our control and will remain out of our control. What we are in control of however, is the direction we are currently moving towards and how quickly we are getting there. Much like on a bumpy road in the outback, if you don't control the wheel then don't blame the road for the destination it brings you to. You can step on the break, slam it into reverse and head in a completely different direction if you choose. So, have the courage not to let yourself drift like so many sadly do, and then get lost in the bushes, take control of your life and progress in the direction you want to go in.

Motivation links

Life is a myriad of experiences; these experiences can be broken down into four categories.

1. Learning
2. Growth
3. Creation
4. Sharing

These will form every experience you will receive throughout your life, in one way or another. The sequence in which these events take place is relatively consistent. First you start in life not knowing anything, so you must learn, through parents, schools, mistakes, lessons, etc. Once you learn skills, you experience growth, in which you expand on those skills and become more proficient in their processes. Then once you master skills, you use those skills to create your existential methods and things that reflect on the things you value and your personality, after that you share what you have created with others and thus make a contribution which gives you meaning and fulfilment. There is no complete monument, masterpiece or accomplishment in today's world that lacks any of these 4 experiences, for you cannot have 1 without the other or any if one is missing. So how does this relate to staying motivated?

The answer is that many people skip a step somewhere, often without their realization. They grow without sufficient learning and try to create their mark, yet don't know how to express themselves and then share it to others not knowing what value exists in it. Many learn but do not grow in that initial learning and create works of an amateur. Some learn, grow, and want to share their growth with the world though never really create themselves. Following these 4 steps, one by one and in their correct order is the only real way to achieve that motivational mark and these are the pillar of motivation as they compound on each other and strengthen the natural bond that exists between them. If you want to stay on top of your motivation game, then learning from the basics is where to start. This will motivate you to learn more and more and grow in your learning potential.

The creative phase happens naturally when intuitively you know that you have learned enough to stand on your own two feet and produce the desire of your work, once you have accomplished this, sharing it with others is again a natural by-product of creativity. The completion of this entire cycle is what serves to motivate others to start their cycles of learning new skills, growing their talents, creating their world, and sharing their creation, which then carries to other people, this is the cycle of motivation and its effects have unlimited potential to change the world for the better.

Who motivates you?

*Your degree of motivation
In anything you do
is related to,
How much of a sense of achievement
you get from what you do,
How much you own what you do,
And how much effort you put into it*
-Dan Ariely 'Payoff'

Achievement

How accomplished do you feel when you achieve someone else's goals? You may feel a sense of it, but it is likely weak and fleeting. If you work in any industry, you are working towards someone else's ideals, whether you like it or not, and this will not give you much if any sense of achievement unless the values expressed by this companies' goals are directly in line with your own.

Ownership

How motivated are you likely to feel if all your creative endeavours and hard work belong to someone else? Likely, not a great deal. Your level of ownership in anything you produce or are involved in directly also have a large impact on how motivated you are in completing that endeavour. If you look at some of the highest quality products on the market today, such as apple products, you will know that their founding member Steve Jobs took complete ownership for his companies' triumphs and downfalls. If you own something, you own it in the good times and bad times alike, and that's the only way you stay motivated enough to improve it, is to own it, and to own it, you have to create it yourself and build it yourself. If you are never motivated in your line of work, consider that. It will likely indicate that you don't own the role you're in. Thus, it has very little meaning to you.

Effort

How good are you likely to feel toward a task you have put minimal effort into? Likely, not a lot. How comfortable are you at handing your work over to someone that is counting on you to produce quality work, yet you just idly scrimped by? This relates to the previous two qualities of ownership and achievement. The more ownership you possess in what you do, the greater the sense of achievement you gain from it, the more effort you will feel compelled to put into it. The fruits of effort you put in is a state of mind and body that cannot be present with mind or body missing from that effort. If you don't have the mental endurance available, it's next to impossible to convince your body to cooperate, likewise if your body is tired, your mind will nag you to put in the opposite of effort, rest. To possess both requires a passion for what you do, period. If you lack passion in the task, your mind will resist, your body will resist, or both will resist in sync, and you will likely come across as lazy, when in fact, you are just not motivated to put in the effort.

We have referred to Steve Jobs several times in this book and we shall again, With Apple being the First Trillion-dollar Company and Steve Jobs being the core of that milestone, what better example to use. So, when it comes to achievement, ownership, and effort, what made Steve Jobs stand mountains above the crowd?

Jobs was driven by great determination and a passion for revolutionizing how the world communicates, watches videos, listens to music, and learn with the aid of a sleek, well-designed, and aesthetically pleasing device that people not only wanted but felt it was an essential part of their identity. Jobs' level of achievement for his products drove his success and motivation each time Apple introduced a new product, and at the forefront of that success was his overflowing passion for his vision to be realized.

Not only was Jobs driven by passion, but he also took complete ownership in his companies' successes and downfalls alike. When sales were down, He worked tirelessly to get to the root cause of the problem; he took responsibility for it and worked at the solution with increased vigour. This sense of achievement could have only been created by the kind of passion that you possess when your business goal is your vision and represents the values that you behold. For Jobs, that was to revolutionize the world, and his success alone is a testament to the power of motivation. The degree of effort Jobs put into his business too was a direct indication to the level of ownership he felt for his brand, often working more than 100 hours a week and well into the early hours of the morning to move a small step forward. His effort was fuelled by his ownership which was a by-product of his achievements, all of which stemmed from his passion and iron belief that he could achieve it.

Steve Jobs was a great innovator and businessman but he did not possess anything that any other person in this world lacks, he just knew the steps it took to get there and was not afraid to take the risks necessary to move above and beyond, a drive that was so strong that it crashed through any obstacle of defeatism that presented itself in any form. Obstacles can be blatantly obvious or subtly sneaky but, in any case, the prepared and strong see through them for what they are and even in some sort of temporary defeat, does not faze this driven person because they see far beyond their vices. Just because you have experienced such short comings, you have to see beyond the initial pain and see the benefit of short-term defeat, the lesson, in which your true motivations reveal themselves. If it is what you really want, no test whether short or long-term will get in the way. The pain-motivation barrier is a test in which so, so, so many people fail in, yet it is perhaps one of the most important tests of all, so then how do we identify and overcome such a common barrier?

The pain-motivation barrier in staying motivated

A slight ache in your joints might not phase you, but if that were to keep getting worse and worse to a stage where it was intolerable, you might think that going to your local GP is merited. Granted, fixing a problem when it is small is great advice, but many in the heat of their flustered lives full of distractions, usually leave every small annoyance until it becomes a hammer to the shin. Motivation is usually low when pain is low so making any changes to improve your situation becomes a low priority; however, fighting the urge to put small issues off is the best way to save yourself not only discomfort now, but potentially serious pain later. Much with any goal you create, you are going to experience some level of discomfort in the present that you will feel compelled to let distract you. That slight push that your mind gives you when you know you're wasting time but continue procrastinating anyway, is like ignoring that minor ache at the start, left unchecked, the pain will grow and grow until the slight push becomes a stampede of charging bulls smashing you out of your comfort zone and into decisive action. It's your choice, you can suffer the pain of discipline and start now while the irritation is only minor, or you can suffer the pain of regret, and realize you've wasted too much time and now have to rush to get things done, and this is not productive. Fight the pain-motivation barrier in its early phases so you can build momentum now and stay motivated while the pain isn't too great.

Have you personally experienced the pain-motivation barrier in any of these areas?

- Sitting around all day for too long, wanting to join a great sporting team to meet new friends only to realize you can't run more than 10 metres without collapsing in exhaustion.

- Eating junk food nearly every meal, not looking after yourself, and then you meet the person of your dreams only to realize they are in great shape and they are not into you because of your lack of self-care
- Going from one meaningless job to another over many years then beating yourself up because you know that's what you never really wanted in the first place
- Never got any great opportunities because you were always afraid to take that initial leap out of your comfort zone.
- Constantly being lost so much in negative thinking, belief systems, and the past that you miss the great moments in life that exist now.

Let me begin by saying I am sure most people can say they have experienced at least one of these pain-motivation barriers in their lives, (and if you haven't, who are you and what is your secret?) Don't beat yourself up, rather learn from these mistakes and let the pain serve to motivate you to not only want and deserve better but to push yourself even harder than before to get it. Pain hurts now, but when you listen to it, and take action to fix the issue, it makes you so much better afterward that you wonder how you would have managed without it. The last thing I want to say is that it is never too late, age is not a denial, status is not a sign of who you are, and where you start in life is your uniqueness. Use these to your advantage and don't try to follow someone else's journey, your motivation will only truly exist if you are already walking on the path, you deem worthy for yourself. You are going to encounter many setbacks, learn from them and keep moving forward, even when you stumble. The spoils belong to he/she who never gives up, who keeps knocking, who keeps seeking and follows their passion if the face of adversity. So, I say to you, start now and don't look back, motivation will continue to grow with you if you choose to keep moving forward one step at a time. Always be moving forward even if they are just baby steps and always strive to be the best version of yourself. I highly encourage you to go over this book as many times as you can and let yourself be constantly reminded that the journey is never really going to be easy, and that is okay, it's the struggles in our journey that make us strong, not the easy times. So be prepared to work harder than ever on your goals and be aware of complacency and time-sapping distractions on your road. Take joy in the fact that you sweat towards success and toil toward fulfillment, there is no other way, just you and all that potential inside of you, so let it out, start now and continue to stay motivated on being who you came here to be.

End of book challenge: Start now. Don't put your goals off any longer. Just start now, no matter how small. If you have started then keep going even if you don't feel like it, push through that resistance and know for yourself the strength that it breathes into you on the other side of the struggle, don't settle for minimal effort and plan your next steps in writing so you have no excuses to get it done.

Don't forget to go over this book again so you can stay on top of your progress and not allow distractions to overwhelm you. Lastly, be honest with yourself and most importantly respect and value the progress you have already made.

The End,
but really only the beginning, your journey has only just begun, there is no end, only another journey waiting for you to start!`

www.ingramcontent.com/pod-product-compliance
Lightning Source LLC
Chambersburg PA
CBHW021448070526
44577CB00002B/303